PRAISE FOR CONSCIOUS CLIENT ATTRACTION

"Attracting clients is important, but attracting the RIGHT clients is a recipe for success. In *Conscious Client Attraction*, Marcia Bench lays out a plan that will ensure you attract the right clients while growing your business in a meaningful way. Be prepared to IGNITE!"

–John Lee Dumas of EOFire.com

"Marcia's approach to client attraction is unique and highly engaging and thoughtful. People buy for emotional reasons and then justify rationally. This book is both spiritual and practical and a great read for anyone wanting to shift to new ways of attracting and working with clients."

–Carolyn Tate, author of *The Purpose Project*
and *Conscious Marketing*

"Finally - someone who understands that manifesting only works when backed with right action! Marcia's unique 'Grounded Woo' style is the perfect blend of proven marketing strategies, amplified by the power of manifestation. If you're here, you've found the right place to achieve your biggest business goals while aligning with the spiritual laws for maximum results."

–Kristin "Rock Your Talk" Thompson, Speaker Trainer
and Coach - SpeakServeGrow.com

"*Conscious Client Attraction* is book that is not just about business, it's about the law of attraction too. Marcia Bench provides a guide for the reader to follow that will allow them to attract more loyal followers. If you are drawn to make a significant impact as a leader in your industry, then this book is a must read!"

–Debbie Allen, Bestselling author of *The Highly Paid Expert*

"This book is written for someone exactly like me, and I bet exactly like you too: spiritual and growth-oriented, yet strategic and success focused. Marcia's expertise shows us that we can be BOTH and don't have to sacrifice success for spiritual growth or personal expansion for revenue. Her decades of experience prove she's the real deal and her systems and strategies work."

– Nancy Marmolejo, TalentAndGenius.com;
Founder of #DeepGenius

"I've known Marcia Bench for 15 years and watched her go from success to success, using her spirituality and well-honed business acumen. In her latest book, *Conscious Client Attraction,* Marcia gives a thorough and empowering roadmap for everyone who wants to create a business and lifestyle that brings them both success and significance. I wish I'd had this book when I started my entrepreneurial journey years ago. Highly recommended.

–Lynne Klippel, best-selling author of *Overcomers, Inc.*
and CEO of LynneKlippel.com

"If you are starting a business or are struggling with your business, this book is a must-read with easy-to-use exercises that will give you the focus, direction and mentoring needed to turn your business around."

–Tammy Washington, Author and Personal Growth Expert

"Wow! I was delightfully surprised that this book gave grounded strategies to attract clients and monetize your special genius. It's pretty much a one-stop shop for any entrepreneur who wants their business to take off!"

–Jeanna Gabellini, co-author
Life Lessons for Mastering the Law of Attraction

"Marcia Bench is a true leader when it comes to conscious business practices and helping conscious-minded entrepreneurs grow their business. *Conscious Client Attraction* is the perfect starting point to building a viable online presence that works for you."

– Tracy Repchuk - TracyRepchuk.com, 7-Time #1 Bestselling author
including *31 Days to Millionaire Marketing Miracles*

"As a professional speaker and coach myself, I was impressed by the clarity and comprehensiveness of Marcia's *Conscious Client Attraction* book. Her work helps professional service providers and experts of all kinds create a message, offer and brand that fully expresses their greatness. The added bonus of up-to-date marketing, energy clearing and manifesting processes make this a must-read for any entrepreneur who wants to grow their business to a global scale.'

–Vanessa Shaw, Business Coach and Mentor

"As a public relations specialist, I know that publicity is only as good as the brand and message behind it. Marcia has laid out a step-by-step roadmap to create a brand that sells - and that can gain the expert the publicity they need for visibility! Then, she helps the reader create media-ready energy by clearing old wounds and being ready to rock-and-roll. A great read, I highly recommend it!"

–Christina Moldenhauer Daves, PR for Anyone

"If that million-dollar check still hasn't shown up in the mail (despite doing affirmations 3 times a day) this book is what you really need. Marcia's 8-Level system has forged real results time after time with entrepreneurs who tried everything and come up short. Or who found success with traditional business tactics that just weren't congruent with who they were at a deep level.

This is a book that meets you where you are. This is not a game of chance, where you place your bets on the consciousness wheel of fortune, give it a spin, and hope you get what you want. It's a reliable system that can deliver, profit, meaning and deep satisfaction. The proof is in the pudding - not only with Marcia's own success, but with dozens of her clients. And this book will help her prove it with you!"

– Rob Schultz, ProfitSeduction.com

CONSCIOUS

CLIENT

ATTRACTION:

8 SIMPLE SECRETS TO BUILDING YOUR EXPERT BUSINESS WHILE NOURISHING YOUR SOUL

MARCIA BENCH

LEADERS IN GLOBAL PUBLISHING

Published by Motivational Press, Inc.
1777 Aurora Road
Melbourne, Florida, 32935
www.MotivationalPress.com

ISBN: 978-1-62865-573-5

CONTENTS

PART 1
THE CONSCIOUS CLIENT ATTRACTION MOVEMENT AND BLUEPRINT

PART 2
IDENTIFYING YOUR CALLING AND MAGNETIC MOVEMENT

PART 3
CREATING YOUR CONSCIOUS BRAND AND OFFER

LIST OF FIGURES

ACKNOWLEDGEMENTS

This book is dedicated to my mother, who passed away while I was writing it. Though we didn't always agree with each other, I could always count on her for support in following my purpose and doing the work I feel called to do. She gave me many gifts – including life itself – and I am grateful to her.

I also want to acknowledge my soulmate and life partner of more than 25 years, Jay. Thank you for always being there with your shining smile and willingness to let me be who I am. Through the ups and downs of being an entrepreneur for most of the time we have been together, you have encouraged me and given me the space I need to fly.

To my publisher, Motivational Press, this is our first foray in partnering together, and I appreciate your patience in giving me more time than I anticipated for this concept to evolve and grow into what it has become within these pages. I look forward to a long and prosperous working relationship.

And of course, I must acknowledge and stop to appreciate the thousands of people who have been part of my work since I began it more than 30 years ago – and especially those who have stepped into the early versions of Conscious Client Attraction to create their own Conscious Expert businesses, with stunning results! Many of their stories are in the book – and you know who you are! Continue to make magic and transform lives.

INTRODUCTION

I am the Marketing and Manifesting Mentor for Conscious Experts.

I am a business healer and rebirther. I help highly skilled experts – and would-be experts - hone in on their life purpose and their ideal business focus, as well as the energy blocks that have kept them from fulfilling that purpose - and then turn it into a thriving, profitable business that changes the world.

I am out to revolutionize the way spiritually-minded entrepreneur experts share their gifts and attract their clients.

I know why you can't do it – why your business isn't responding to your relentless wishing and hoping it could change or to your pursuit of "Bright Shiny Objects…"

Because simply pursuing one strategy after another, one new offering after another, and one business design after another, simply won't work. Dabbling in your spare time watching free videos, wishing you could join the ranks of the six– and seven- figure-earning experts, will not get you there.

Success as a leader, coach, entrepreneur or expert is not just about strategy.

It's not just about sitting on a mountaintop and meditating to manifest your dreams.

It's not just about fulfilling your life purpose.

And it's definitely not about ignoring the inner pain and the resulting energy blocks created by your life setbacks.

It's about getting all of these working together – in the right proportion, like a perfect recipe for your favorite dish.

WHO CAN BENEFIT

Over the last three decades of my career, I have had the opportunity to work with a widely diverse client base. They usually have a great deal of success in their background, and other people think they have it all together - but inside they know there is a new part of themselves wanting to emerge. It is both exciting and frightening at the same time. You too can benefit from the life-changing Conscious Client Attraction approach if you are like these people whom I continue to attract to this work.

You might be a seasoned executive experiencing a newfound spiritual awareness, a healer who has been unable to get her business off the ground, or an author who just wrote a book and is thinking "now what? The book is published – so how do I make money from it?" Rest assured, Conscious Client Attraction can help you.

Perhaps you are a coach who just graduated coaching school with flying colors, but they didn't teach you how to market yourself to get clients and make money with your coaching. Or you may be a professional speaker who is tired of being a "road warrior," trading time for dollars and dealing with the increasing inconveniences of air travel – and you long for life balance, freedom, and an online business you love.

My clients have been people just like you, often very accomplished professionals with multiple degrees, who still can't figure out why they can't launch or scale their businesses.

Lynne was a former school principal and university professor turned healer who was making a fraction of her prior income when she came to me – and working only one-on-one with clients, providing services completely customized to each client's needs. I helped her hone her market, streamline her service delivery, start charging higher fees and make offers from her speeches. She has already had three record-breaking months this year – and the year is only halfway over!

Then there was Melissa, who, despite her two decades of recruiting and resume writing background, was struggling to attract enough clients when she started working with me. By truly owning her uniqueness and designing a high-impact career coaching system for executives, she began attracting dozens of new clients every month. She is now scaling her offerings to help sustain her two-location lifestyle and enjoy the frequent vacations and travel she loves.

WHY THIS WILL WORK WHEN OTHER BOOKS/PROGRAMS HAVEN'T

Even if you are brand new to entrepreneurship, I'll be you have spent hours watching YouTube videos promising the key to success and profit. And if you've had your business for a while, you've probably hired at least one business coach.

But the problem with so many coaches, mentors and programs is that they help you in only one dimension of your needs. They help you clarify your purpose and mission – but they don't help you turn it into a viable business.

Or they help you heal your energy wounds and transform your beliefs - but they don't give you an actionable business growth strategy.

Or maybe they teach you manifesting principles - but they don't help you turn those principles into clients on your calendar and dollars in your bank account.

The Conscious Client Attraction Blueprint is unique in that it is four-dimensional. You first clarify your Divine Work and gifts – including your Chakra Business Type. Then, secondly, we help you clear the energy blocks that have kept you from fully expressing it in the world. And it doesn't stop there! The third element is the Laws of Creation that actually work – and that I've been personally using in my own business and with clients for more than three decades. Finally, we give you a paint-by-numbers business branding, marketing and growth strategy that resonates deep within your soul – and with the thousands of ideal clients you are intended to serve.

Why get only a couple of the ingredients of that cake you want to bake – when you can have the whole thing? That's what Conscious Client Attraction is about.

This is not an empty promise; you can do this!

I'VE BEEN THERE...I KNOW WHAT IT'S LIKE TO DENY YOUR TRUE SELF!

A book like this can't come from just theory – it must be birthed through the fires of personal experience.

I grew up in a fundamentalist religious household, where intuition was frowned upon and negative emotions were stifled. I was taught to follow the rules and obey those in authority – so I did. I tried the path of secretarial school my parents wanted me to take, but it left me unfulfilled.

So I returned to college to become the first in my family to complete a college degree – and in the process, also left my childhood religion behind. It no longer fit!

Then, I went to work as support staff in a law firm, later deciding to follow the logical path of becoming a lawyer instead of the heart path and calling I felt to further my education in psychology.

I cut my hair super short, got some navy blue business suits – even scarves tied like a bow tie! – trying to fit into the male-dominated corporate and legal world. I denied my intuition, my spiritual growth, and my femininity to "get ahead." The presentations I gave were loaded with information, but lacked impact.

I knew something was missing. But I was afraid if I revealed the importance of my spiritual path and my meditation practices to my clients, my audiences and my fellow attorneys, they would think less of me, call me "woo woo," or doubt my credibility.

Even after I became a certified coach, I continued to largely deny the spiritual aspects of myself and the work I did – until I could no longer hold back.

I traveled to the mountaintops of Colorado to study with a shaman, read books on healing, studied energy, angels, the chakras, numerology, crystals, tapping, visioning, and affirmations, I pursued anything I could find that would help me access the hidden dimension of life – and in turn, business.

Then, I began sharing those tools with my clients, in my presentations, and even "channeled" one of my books.

And guess what? People began seeking me out *because* I blended spirituality and business – not in spite of it! I knew in principle that it should work that way – but it was not until I actually started being authentic and vulnerable that I was able to see the manifesting in action.

My clothing went from business suits to flowy clothing, and then settled somewhere in between. I even performed some healing work at a live event I hosted – with amazing results!

So if you're a "closet woo-woo" executive or professional now, I know how painful it can be to deny the essence of who you are in order to try to fit into the mainstream business world.

Thankfully, as we'll see in chapter 1, that's no longer a requirement in today's world of evolving consciousness! In fact, if business and financial success has eluded you – or you have just felt unfulfilled and known something was missing - it will be in the revealing of your hidden Self that you will find that missing piece.

The best part is, once you make the leap to start your own business as a Conscious Expert – or use what you learn in this book to restructure your current business to give you more freedom and allow for more growth – you will enjoy lifestyle benefits of which most people only dream. You can work from home, instead of suffering through a daily commute. You can work only a few hours a week, instead of having only a few hours a week left for yourself. You can choose your own clients, instead of tolerating an incompetent boss. You can blow the lid off your income ceiling, while becoming highly respected and well-known for triumphing over the very things you might currently see as your biggest setbacks. Read the stories that follow, and build or rebuild your business foundation, step-by-step. And be sure to access the resources we have compiled online at marciabench.com/cca-book-resources to help you.

HOW THIS BOOK IS ORGANIZED

This book is organized into five Parts.

Part 1, The Conscious Client Attraction Movement and Blueprint, begins with one chapter outlining the background of the Conscious Client Attraction Movement and our Blueprint. You will learn how it was developed, and why it is needed now. We give you many reasons why it's critical for you to join us and use it as the foundation for your business.

Then, in chapter two, we explore the four key ingredients of the Conscious Client Attraction model: 1: Calling – Your Soul's Purpose and Passionate Expression (Your "GPS Setting"), 2: Chakras – Your Inner Energy Roadmap; 3: Creative Laws – the Rules of the Road for Manifesting, and 4: Conscious Business Strategy – Your Outer Roadmap.

In Part 2, Identifying Your Calling and Magnetic Movement, we help you hone in on and clarify some of the fundamental building blocks of your Conscious Expert business, including Your Conscious Purpose, Mission, and Vision, and your Consciously Defined Movement & Micro-Niche – the unique subset of the overall population that is perfectly matched to the services you offer.

In Part 3, Creating Your Conscious Brand and Offer, you will mine your past wounds and triumphs to find the golden nuggets, and turn those into a Conscious Signature System. You can use this now to serve more individual clients and, later, to scale your business, income and offerings. Chapter 6 guides you through how to package your services and price them.

In Part 4, Connecting with Your Tribe, you take the work you did in parts 2 and 3 in putting your brand offerings together and now begin your

Conscious Communication and Outreach. This is where you actually engage with your prospective clients, both online and offline. Chapter 8 helps you both hold the right energy and ask the right questions to turn Conscious Conversations into Clients.

Finally, Part 5 explores Delivering Your Gifts and Growing Your Business. Client enrollment doesn't end when the client says yes! It's critical that you build on that commitment by providing exceptional Conscious Customer Care – and create a WOW experience for your new and existing clients. In a world where people feel increasingly anonymous and like a cog in the wheel when interacting with their service providers, you can create a unique advantage just by putting more focus on your client care!

Then, looking toward the future, chapter 10 helps you see a vision for Conscious Business & Movement Expansion and Growth. How big do you want to grow your business, your income, and your impact? How much change do you want to facilitate in the world? What is the best structure to use to do this?

We end with an Epilogue exploring next steps: Where do we take the movement from here? We suggest practical ways you can implement Conscious Client Attraction and get support.

PART 1

THE CONSCIOUS CLIENT ATTRACTION MOVEMENT AND BLUEPRINT

CHAPTER 1

WHAT CONSCIOUS CLIENT ATTRACTION IS & WHY NOW

WHAT YOU'LL LEARN IN THIS CHAPTER

- Are You a Conscious Expert?
- How Consciousness Has Evolved to Set the Stage for Your Work
- How the Entrepreneur Movement's Explosion Works in Your Favor
- The Connection Between Purpose and Conscious Client Attraction
- The 8 Core Conscious Client Attraction Principles

More people are starting their own businesses now than at any other time in history.

After all, you can put up a website overnight and call yourself a coach, a healer, an author, or a speaker. Or you can sell a product online or resell others' products and services – all from the comfort of your home.

But the tried-and-true statistic that 85 percent of new businesses fail within the first two years is not only still true – the time to failure now is more like three to six months.

Why?

Because the content often lacks what I refer to as "consciousness." Many of today's online businesses are the equivalent of a "get rich quick" scheme. In contrast, a Conscious Expert business is an inspired, strategically planned, and intentionally created organism that generates a buzz, a movement, and a following of people who are eager to build and deepen an ongoing relationship with you, not just to complete a transaction.

ARE YOU A CONSCIOUS EXPERT?

WHY "CONSCIOUS" CLIENT ATTRACTION

The time has come to recognize that the Information Economy has run its course, and we are now entering the Attraction Economy. Drawing clients to our businesses is not just a game of strategy– it requires tapping into the energy of our offer, our prospect, and the entire process by which we bring them into our business.

Our prospective clients – and consumers as a whole – are much more sophisticated than they were 15 years ago. Companies bombard them with more than 5,000 marketing messages daily. And because they can't process anywhere near that much information, our prospects have trained themselves to see right through canned approaches, manipulative or aggressive marketing messages, and lack of authenticity on any level.

It is refreshing to meet someone who has a service to offer that is valuable to me as a consumer, especially if it doesn't have a hidden agenda. The provider simply begins a conversation, and if there is a potential fit, they guide the conversation along to help me make the right decision.

WHY NOW

It is not just because our prospective clients' tolerance for aggressive marketing has lessened that the timing is now right for Conscious Client Attraction. The entire dynamic of how people find and invest in professional services has been turned on its ear.

Think about the last time you wanted to find a manicurist, a hotel, a tutor for your children, or a consultant for your business. Did you pull out the most recent direct mail pieces from the firms that have contacted you recently to make your choice? Did you look in the Yellow Pages?

No – chances are you sought a referral first, and asked friends and colleagues if they had used a similar service. After that you might have gone to your favorite social media platform to ask your connections. Or you might go to Google or yelp and search for that kind of professional to find people near you that could meet your needs, right? And once you get one or two names to consider, you then research them online before contacting them, correct?

It is no different with your services. For people to find you, you need to be findable. You need to be seen in the places where they are looking when they're ready for someone like you. Sometimes they have a need, but haven't yet turned it into an active search. You also want to be seen by them when they are searching so you can continue a dialogue with them and be the one that they select when it's time to buy.

The secret does not lie only in search engine optimization or Facebook ads – although those might be part of your process later on. The secret is knowing exactly what problem you solve, who can most benefit from your solution, and where they hang out. Then you need to know how to enter the dialogue they are already having in their mind during their search. That is what Conscious Client Attraction is all about.

Fig. 1 contains our quiz to see if you are one of the people we include in the term "Conscious Expert."

Right now we are seeing a perfect storm of three primary trends that make it the perfect time to launch and grow your Conscious Expert business:

1. Consciousness

2. Entrepreneurship (especially among experts).

3. Purpose.

We'll explore each in turn.

FIG. 1 QUIZ: ARE YOU A CONSCIOUS EXPERT?

	Question	Yes	No
1	Have you overcome a tragedy, illness or other situation and discovered a solution that others could benefit from?		
2	Do you have a passion about helping others through the work you do?		
3	Do you dream about having a global following of people who want to work with you?		
4	Do you love giving presentations, and long to present your own content powerfully to people who understand you?		
5	Do you wish you could write your own book?		
6	Do you feel like you have a deep soul calling to help others transform their lives?		
7	Are you drawn to one or more spiritual practices that help you find comfort, feel grounded and make sense of life?		
8	Are you willing to continue working on yourself to heal your past and create your ideal future, so you can better serve your clients?		
Score			

TREND #1: HOW CONSCIOUSNESS HAS EVOLVED TO SET THE STAGE FOR YOUR WORK

THE MEANING BEHIND "CONSCIOUS"

To many people, "conscious" simply means intentional or deliberate; on purpose. The dictionary defines it as, "fully aware of or sensitive to something."

Certainly, being conscious in the sense of being deliberate, aware, and intentional about what we offer, to whom we offer it and how we attract people to our work is a step in the right direction!

But it's not enough. We are using the term to mean bringing a *higher* consciousness to your business as a Conscious Expert, more akin to how that term is used in philosophy and some spiritual traditions.

To be conscious in our context means:

- Bringing a higher consciousness to everything we do.

- Being fully awakened to and enlivened by our calling and our purpose – and building our expert business around it.

- Always expanding our awareness of the energy we bring to our life and our business, then healing and transforming any blocks to clear our energy.

- Recognizing the oneness of all beings – including us and our clients/followers – and drawing our ideal clients to us by being that which we wish to attract.

- Realizing that what we do, say and think as individuals reflects and magnifies in the world – and deliberately choosing our actions, words and thoughts to contribute to a higher consciousness in the world.

Until recently, understanding and using consciousness principles was confined to followers of Eastern philosophy and certain religions. But as we will see in a moment, the Attraction Economy invites it into the mainstream.

THE HISTORY OF CONSCIOUSNESS

While we could go all the way back to the time B.C. (Before Christ) to track the journey of consciousness, that is not necessary for our purposes here.

Many people believe that the Law of Attraction was born when the movie "The Secret" was released in 2006. But we can trace its roots back at least 100 years before that. (We could even argue that some of the principles in Jesus' Sermon on the Mount promulgated the idea that like attracts like.)

In the early 1900s, thought leaders, such as Doctor Ernest Holmes, Doctor Phineas Quimby, Thomas Troward, and Charles and Myrtle Fillmore, among others, began speaking and writing about Creation Laws.

Later, Napoleon Hill was commissioned by Andrew Carnegie to study the 100 greatest industrialists of the post-Depression era and share their principles for success in his book, *Think and Grow Rich*. Much of what he teaches in that book – which is the second best-selling book of all time next to the Bible – is all about having a vision and tapping into the Creation Laws to materialize it.

In the 1980's, author/consultant Laura Day brought intuition into the boardroom - and it hasn't left. Rick Warren's *The Purpose Driven Life* sold 60 million copies and was on the bestseller list for more than 90 weeks.

Hay House was one of the first publishing houses to feature authors and speakers specializing in these topics. I feel very fortunate to be one of the first three authors they published, besides the late Louise Hay herself. They now run events all over the world called You Can Do It! These events are attended by thousands of people seeking additional guidance on manifesting and related topics. These topics are essential parts of the Conscious Client Attraction method.

Simultaneously, as more women have entered the world of commerce and become primary breadwinners for their family, they have demanded that the marketing and sales process change. They now influence 85% of buying decisions of everything from automobiles to houses, groceries to beauty products. The rise of the Divine Feminine energy in commerce, as well as in our overall consciousness, is apparent as we see more and more focus on "both and" instead of "either or" options. Leadership increasingly favors collaboration over competition and inclusivity instead of exclusivity. Inc. Magazine reports that 88% of Millennial workers prefer collaborative environments over competitive ones.

The industry of coaching has created a growing number of entrepreneurs with a higher consciousness. The industry began in 1989, under the guidance of the late Thomas Leonard. Many life coaches began helping people discover what their purpose in life was and how it impacted their current lifestyle and decisions. Many were trained directly in the laws of attraction. The industry has continued to grow since that time to now several hundred thousand people worldwide, and hundreds of coach training programs in existence.

Another movement that has begun to integrate purpose and other aspects of consciousness into business – especially larger companies – is the Conscious Capitalism movement. Cofounded by business professor Raj Sisodia and John Mackey of Whole Foods in 2010, they define Conscious Capitalism as "a way of thinking about capitalism and business that better reflects where we are in the human journey, the state of our world today, and the innate potential of business to have a positive impact on world." Its four tenets include higher purpose and core values, stakeholder integration, conscious leadership, and conscious culture and management. As Conscious Experts, we can learn a lot from a philosophy of Conscious Capitalism, even though many of its principles apply primarily to larger companies.

Coming along shortly after the Conscious Capitalism movement and its 2014 book was Australian author Carolyn Tate's *Conscious Marketing*. She applies consciousness principles to marketing approaches companies can use. She defines conscious marketing this way: "Conscious marketing is all about building something so fundamentally good and compelling right into the heart of your business, products and services that everyone… wants to join your Tribe and spread the word."

Conscious Client Attraction builds in these ideas and adds another dimension by bringing higher consciousness to Conscious Experts in their business launches, marketing and growth. We use the Creation Laws with proven principles of marketing, as well as the roadmap of the eight chakras or energy centers.

See Fig. 2 for a timeline of how consciousness has evolved to set the stage for your work.

FIG. 2: TIMELINE OF CONSCIOUSNESS AND THE CONSCIOUS CLIENT ATTRACTION MOVEMENT

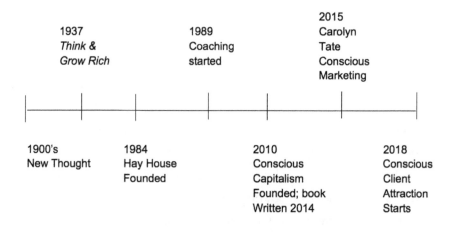

TREND #2: HOW THE ENTREPRENEUR MOVEMENT'S EXPLOSION WORKS IN YOUR FAVOR

ENTREPRENEURSHIP AS A FORCE

The first aspect of entrepreneurship to note is its sheer numbers. There are approximately 25 million small businesses in the U.S. (defined by the Small Business Administration as less than 500 employees), generating more than 75 percent of the Gross National Product. The Kauffman Institute reports that after dipping to their lowest point in 2011, the number of start-ups now exceeds the rates prior to the Great Recession of

2008. Women have been starting businesses at two to three times the rate of men for decades.

But the reality in most jurisdictions is that at least half to two-thirds of these are "micropreneurs," meaning they consist of one primary business owner working from a home base with virtual, contracted staff. This is the fastest growing sector within the entrepreneur movement.

The globalization of the Internet since its invention in 1989 has made starting a business as easy as putting up a website – crowding the market with thousands of services and marketing messages. Therefore, while the good news is that it is easier than ever to start an expert business and create an online presence, business owners are facing increased skepticism among their prospective clients. This makes it harder than ever to sell using the old methods. Entrepreneurs must embrace Conscious Client Attraction principles to be successful in this changing market.

A 2016 study by HSBC Bank found that 64% of the entrepreneurs surveyed believe it is their duty to have a positive social and economic impact on society. Seventy-four percent gave to good causes in the preceding year.

THE PROFESSIONAL SPEAKING INDUSTRY POST-RECESSION

The second aspect of the expert industry that trends in your favor is the professional speaking industry. Prior to the 2008 Recession, companies and conventions commonly hired keynote speakers and motivational speakers for their events, and paid them thousands of dollars for an hour-long speech.

This all came to a screeching halt when the 2008 Recession hit. One of the first things companies scrapped was bringing in fee–paid speakers for their events. Instead, they began to demand that speakers not only entertain, but also educate – and so the term "edutainment" was born. Many speakers began to embrace the Speak-to-Sell model instead, where they covered their own expenses to do a free talk for an audience of qualified prospects, made an offer from stage and took orders at the back of the room. A third model of speaking called the Sponsorship Model then emerged. Here, when the speaker wants to address a qualified audience, they are required to pay several thousand dollars as a sponsor fee to the host of the event to do so. This is still common practice today.

Companies are now much more focused on getting in ROI on the investment they make by bringing in a speaker. Not only are there fewer paid speaking engagements, but to qualify for them, you must show the substantive value of what you are going to deliver, and be able to edutain the audience. Most speakers also negotiate follow-on coaching, product sales or training beyond the initial speech, both to increase results from their presentation and for additional streams of income to their business.

Corporations continue to invest more than $16 billion per year in training for their employees. And you can become part of their stable of trainers with the right message. There are more than 77,000 meetings every day in North America. The biggest complaint heard from meeting planners is that they are still having trouble finding interesting, engaging speakers that have great content. So once you have developed your conscious message, there is an ongoing market for it.

Not only are there in-person speaking opportunities, but you can literally create your own media empire with no limitations whatsoever. You can host a podcast that gets distributed through iTunes, film live videos on Facebook or YouTube and send traffic to them, or even create your own documentary or online television talk show. In the future, online media may become regulated; but right now is a golden opportunity to become the "Kardashians" of your Tribe (so to speak). Therefore, if online media becomes regulated in the future, you are still an icon with a public presence to leverage.

BOOK PUBLISHING TODAY

The third segment of the expert entrepreneur industry that works to your advantage as a Conscious Expert is book publishing. While we still have the big five publishing houses that only accept authors through an agent, a large percentage of the more than 200,000 books published every year are self-published. Services like Amazon's CreateSpace, coupled with virtual distributors and fulfillment houses like Vervante.com, make it easy for authors to publish their own books and promote them on social media and other online portals – as well as through their own speaking - instead of relying on the Madison Avenue publishers for their golden opportunity.

And while writing a book cannot be relied upon as your claim to fame, it can be a wonderful vehicle through which your prospects can learn more about you before they explore your services. It also provides you with tremendous credibility when seeking speaking engagements, and becomes the "bible" of your movement.

Programs like Brendon Burchard's Expert Academy, our Conscious Experts Academy events, and many other training events occur literally daily to serve the growing market of online entrepreneur experts. However, it is the buyer who must sift and sort to determine whose service to invest in – and whether it is sound and will help them reach their desired result.

In short, being a Conscious Expert in today's economy puts you in a place of being sought-after and known in ways that were virtually impossible even a decade ago.

TREND #3: THE PURPOSE MOVEMENT

The final trend that coalesces with consciousness and entrepreneurship in setting the stage for your work is the Purpose Movement. When I began my first business in 1986, the idea of discovering and following your life purpose was just beginning to be discussed. Books such as Nancy Anderson's *Work with Passion* and Marsha Sinetar's *Do What You Love and the Money will Follow*, as well as Joseph Campbell's PBS series on the Hero's Journey and following your bliss, led the charge.

Now, as we will see below, an increasing number of companies are doing the work to determine their own purpose as a company, and to help their employees discover and fulfill their individual purposes through the company and their work there. So if you've been feeling the emergence of your life purpose for the first time, or sense a new way in which it wants to express, you are right on target with the work you are meant to be doing. We will explore life purpose in greater detail in chapter 3.

MY LIFE PURPOSE JOURNEY

When I was 14 years old, just a year after my dad had passed away at age 37 from brain cancer, I began questioning the meaning of life. Maybe I had always been asking the tough questions – my mom gave me a book trying to answer those questions when I was a young child. But neither the answers my parents gave, my ministers gave, or my teachers gave seemed to satisfy me. I had a burning awareness that I was here for reason and that I had important work to do in the world. However, since I have varying interests and many talents – as I'm sure you do – it became increasingly difficult to hone in on what that purpose was.

I took classes, went to seminars, read books, and asked people that I thought should know how to find my purpose – and still couldn't figure it out. Every job I had became unchallenging and boring after just a few months. There was no longer any challenge, and I had no other reason to stay – so I changed jobs frequently. I was in and out of college and law school for 10 years getting my two degrees. Studying psychology definitely helped, but I still felt like my life purpose eluded me. The journey continued for a total of 18 years.

Finally, once I finished law school, and then – importantly – started my first business part-time on the side, I knew I had found my purpose. Going into business as a Conscious Expert changed my life. I put together some exercises and tools I had learned along the way and began teaching those in seminars and workshops. Later, I created a career discovery model, based on my journey, and later began certifying coaches in this model through my coach training company – virtually inventing the niche of career coaching. That in turn evolved to what I do now, helping Conscious Experts discover their life purpose and create a business around it.

PURPOSE IN BUSINESS IS GROWING

The great news is the Purpose Movement is penetrating all sectors of business today, including the coaching industry. I remember the first time I spoke at a national career development gathering and recommended that practitioners explore life purpose with their clients, not just administer assessments and focus on skills. If the members of the audience had had rotten tomatoes, they probably would have thrown them at me.

Now, when I attend the same conference, the evolution is obvious. While they certainly have not abandoned assessments and skills evaluation, conversations about purpose and passion are common.

In *Path to Purpose,* William Damon writes,

"Purpose is a stable and generalized intention to accomplish something that is at the same time meaningful to the self and consequential for the world beyond the self."

That is the beauty of bringing the idea of purpose into business. It merges the desire of the self for creative expression with a need in the world for a specific change. It reminds me of the Japanese concept of Ikigai, depicted in Fig. 3.

FIG. 3 IKIGAI ("A REASON FOR BEING")

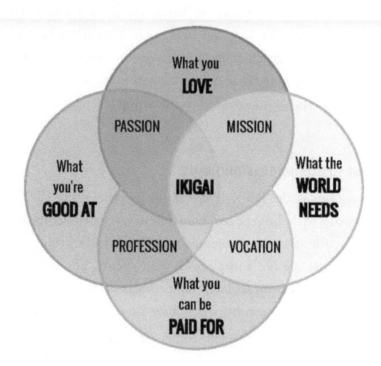

When the things you love, what you're good at, what you can be paid for and what the world needs intersect, everyone benefits.

In *Conscious Capitalism,* the authors state their purpose in writing the book as "to inspire the creation of more conscious businesses: businesses galvanized by higher purposes that serve and align the interest of all their major stakeholders…" Some of the companies who embrace Conscious Capitalism and purpose in their business include, Southwest Airlines, Whole Foods, Ebay, Johnson& Johnson, Jet Blue, Starbucks, and more. So the notion of pursuing one's purpose is not just for Conscious Experts – big business is embracing it too!

The *Conscious Capitalism* authors point out that "when businesspeople operate with a low level of consciousness about the purpose and impact of business, they engage in trade-off thinking that creates many harmful, unintended consequences."

If you have ever worked in a government setting, or another large corporation with a widespread entitlement mentality, you know what this quote is referring to. Employees are there physically, but not in spirit – getting by, and doing as little as possible to earn a paycheck. Perhaps that is why you are reading this book – you have been there and done that and want to transcend that mentality by sharing your unique gifts with an audience that is eager to receive them.

Aaron Hurst and his company Imperative have even developed a Purpose Employer Audit to lay out the full picture of what a purpose-driven human resources approach looks like. (See imperative.com for details.)

People are hungry for purpose and meaning. Your quest for your own purpose is a hologram of what your future Tribe is seeking. As you mine your talents and gifts, as well as your own purpose, and turn them into a thriving business, you will inspire many others to do the same.

THE 8 CORE CONSCIOUS CLIENT ATTRACTION PRINCIPLES

Conscious Client Attraction emerges as the solution that frustrated customers and would-be experts alike are seeking. It galvanizes the lessons learned during the Recession, as well as the trends in the areas of consciousness, entrepreneurship and purpose. It provides you with an approach to crafting your business and brand, and then disseminating your message and gifts as broadly as you wish.

We define Conscious Client Attraction as a four-dimensional model for building a Conscious Expert business, in which:

(a) You first clarify your Divine Work and gifts.

(b) You clear the energy blocks that have kept you from fully expressing it in the world.

(c) You use the Creation Laws to accelerate your results.

(d) You implement 8 key steps to crafting your message and offer (steps 1 through 4) and connecting with your ideal clients to serve them (steps 5 through 8) in a way that resonates deep within your soul – and with the thousands of ideal clients you are intended to serve.

Following are the core principles or "secrets" for each aspect of Conscious Client Attraction that we will be discussing in depth throughout the rest of the book.

Secret 1: Conscious Experts have a vision for the business that is long-term, not just short-term. They know what the business is here to do. Conscious businesses have a purpose that flows from the heart and soul of the founder/owner. The business fulfills his/her life purpose – and that of its stakeholders – by its very being. Using the Creation Laws, visualizations and affirmations alone is not enough to build a successful business. Neither is marketing strategy alone enough – both are needed. If one is blocked or misaligned internally, changing marketing strategy will not markedly change the results until the energy block is healed and aligned.

Secret 2: General offerings no longer work – today we must communicate what we offer as a specific problem to be solved for specific audience in a way that is unique to us – a Micro-niche. A business which first has a compelling purpose creates a magnetic movement that irresistibly attracts people to its Tribe. They want to be a part of the movement, partly due to Fear of Missing Out (FOMO). The mission and movement of a business are determined from the inside out, not by simply looking at the marketplace and choosing based on what will sell the most. The legacy of the business is formed through a combination of effectively communicating what the magnetic movement stands for, and then structuring its services to expand that movement.

Secret 3: Conscious Experts know the importance of becoming known for something important – their Conscious Signature System, which leaves their mark and their legacy on the planet. This system outlines a transformational process, mirroring the Hero's Journey, that clients of the business can implement, with predictable, replicable results. This Conscious Signature System is embedded in every offering and price point.

Secret 4: Conscious Experts may start out enrolling and working one-on-one with individual clients, but as their movement grows, they expand to offer leveraged group offerings to serve a larger Tribe. The Conscious Expert's service packages, all based on their Conscious Signature System, range in price from free to 5- and 6-figures. Each price point provides increasing levels of access to the Conscious Expert.

Secret 5: Conscious businesses know that today's consumers have become immune to generalized, manipulative, and inauthentic marketing. They know it is possible to attract clients and customers in a way that builds a meaningful relationship - not just the completion of a transaction. Conscious Experts are aware that each communication they and their team members have – whether in person, by phone, online or otherwise – carries the energy of its movement with it, and they are mindful of each interaction. They cultivate an awareness of the energy they bring to each interaction, as well as the energy that each prospect and client carries, and how to communicate authentically over all platforms and media.

Secret 6: The customer will invest in the services they need – even if it is a significant stretch financially – if they believe in the movement that the Conscious Expert stands for and also believes that they are the right provider for them. Enrolling clients into your movement and inviting them to buy from you is all about connecting to their "why." The Conscious Expert then guides them through a conversation that makes the solution irresistible and inevitable.

Secret 7: Conscious Experts know that the sale does not end when the client or customer pays. It is simply the beginning of a sacred connection that continues with Conscious Customer Care. It is no longer enough to merely meet the basic standard expected by the client in delivering one's services. Over-delivering, going above and beyond, and making sure they have support as close to 24 hours a day as possible are all components of a wow conscious customer experience.

Secret 8: What got you here will not get you to the next level in your business. The Conscious Expert is always seeking out mentorship, personal growth, further clarification of his or her personal purpose, and guidance in how best to spread the movement while staying out of its way. Conscious Experts know that as the movement and business grows, their role will change and expand. They allow the organic growth of the business through all the stages of its life, including implementing the staff and systems that support that growth.

Let's get started bringing these principles to life in your business!

CHAPTER 2

THE FOUR KEY INGREDIENTS – AND WHY THEY ARE ESSENTIAL TO YOUR SUCCESS AS AN ENTREPRENEUR

WHAT YOU'LL LEARN IN THIS CHAPTER

- The Four Key Ingredients of Conscious Client Attraction
- Following Your Calling
- Your Chakra System
- How to Use the Creation Laws in Your Business
- The Conscious Business Strategy
- The 8 Chakra Business Types

Now that we know that Conscious Client Attraction is a movement whose time has come, let's look at the four key ingredients that will help it come alive for you. Then, you can reach the exciting goals you have for your business, while staying fully aligned within yourself.

THE FOUR KEY INGREDIENTS OF CONSCIOUS CLIENT ATTRACTION

Remember, building your business is like baking a cake: without any one of the four key ingredients, you will get a result – but it won't look or taste like the picture on the box!

As depicted in Fig. 4, the four key ingredients are:

1 – Calling – Your Soul's Purpose & Passionate Expression (Your "GPS Setting")

2 – Chakras – Your Inner Energy Roadmap

3 – Creation Laws – The Rules of The Road for Manifesting

4 – Conscious Business Strategy – Your Outer Roadmap

FIG. 4 - 4 INGREDIENTS OF CONSCIOUS CLIENT ATTRACTION

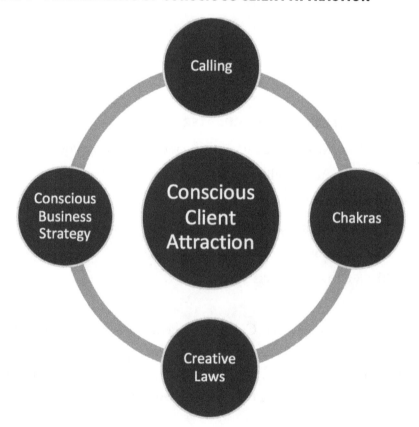

1. FOLLOWING YOUR CALLING

Perhaps, like me, you felt at an early age that you had important work to do on the planet. Or, you might be realizing that following a pivotal life event or one of those birthdays ending in zero!

I believe each one of us is here with a specific life purpose, and until our work expresses that purpose, something will be lacking. If I were to ask you whether or not your current work or business expresses your life purpose, what would your answer be? Don't overthink it - your initial impression is correct.

Think of your calling as the GPS setting for your life. Just as when you get in the car, you input an address and ask the GPS service to guide you there, your calling provides that kind of direction in your life. How do you choose that direction? You follow your passion or, as Joseph Campbell put it, you follow your bliss.

Here are some of the questions you will find yourself asking when you are seeking to define your calling.

- What is the purpose of my life?
- Why am I here?
- What kind of work or business would fulfill me?
- What am I meant to do?
- How can I feel more sense of meaning about what I do every day?
- What is the next step in my soul's evolution?

Your search for your calling may be the reason you picked up this book. It is the primary reason that I do the work I do – because I spent the first 32 years of my life not knowing how to answer the questions above. I know what it feels like not to know your calling, and I know the incredible sense of fulfillment that comes once you do.

Don't worry – we're going to delve into this topic in-depth in chapter 3. Whether or not you feel clear on your calling now, it is key that you get clear on what it is, and how it desires to express now. Then you can ensure that you, your business direction and focus, and your clients will all be heading towards that same goal.

2. YOUR CHAKRA SYSTEM

Hidden within you is an energy roadmap that can either illuminate your path or block the way. Which way that roadmap impacts you depends on whether each center is able to freely circulate the available energy, or whether past wounds in your life restrict it.

The word "chakra" literally means "wheel" in Sanskrit. And while the chakras cannot be viewed with the eyes in the sense a spleen or liver or lungs can, they are visible to those who have the gift of clairvoyance. Certain healers and intuitives have that gift.

The Eastern mystics have mapped the 7 most commonly referenced chakras as depicted in Fig. 5, The Chakra System:

FIG. 5 THE CHAKRA SYSTEM

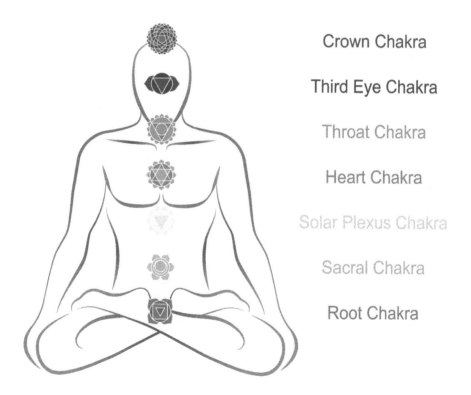

Crown Chakra

Third Eye Chakra

Throat Chakra

Heart Chakra

Solar Plexus Chakra

Sacral Chakra

Root Chakra

The 8th chakra is your aura, which surrounds your body about four feet in all directions, and is visible through aura photography or by clairvoyant individuals.

Whether our life is going well or poorly, the colors in our aura and the functioning of our chakras reflect it. When we have something happen that is traumatic, such as the death of a loved one, a bad breakup, a physical disease, or hurtful words spoken repeatedly to us, they create a kind of "energetic scar tissue" in the chakra related to that issue. Each trauma in a particular center further restricts the circulation of energy, until the person feels either emotionally shut down, manifests a physical illness or disease, or simply becomes numb.

You may think the verbal abuse by a parent in your childhood or the unfaithfulness of a spouse two years ago has nothing to do with whether or not your business will succeed – but it does. Everything is connected. We see it tangibly in the world of economics – a massive stock market downturn in the United States causes uncertainty in other global markets too. Not quite as obvious is the fact that each of our personal relationships, mindsets, beliefs, and attitudes lead to our actions and the words we speak. Those in turn, affect others around us and the global consciousness as a whole.

Watch what happens when the CEO walks through the pool of workers on the way to his or her office, looking down and greeting no one, versus their normal personal outreach to each of the valued employees. That will create a wave of unsettledness among the staff, and may also cause them to act similarly aloof – or even angry – with others in their life because of their fear.

There's a story that is told of a grandfather whose four-year-old grandson kept asking him questions and wanting to play, but the grandfather just didn't want to right then. So he pulled out a picture of the earth and tore it into 20 or 30 small pieces. As he mixed them up and handed them to the grandson, he asked the grandson to go to his room and put the pieces back together. He thought that would keep him busy at least for the rest of the day.

A little over an hour later, and the grandson proudly came back to the grandfather and said, "Here you go!" The grandfather was stunned to see that the little boy had correctly put together the entire earth, with all of the countries of the right places, in such a short time. He asked his grandson, "How did you do that so quickly?" The grandson replied, "Well, I noticed that on the other side there was a picture of a man. Once I put the man back together, the world came back together too."

What a beautiful metaphor for each of us. By putting ourselves back together, as we heal and clear our past wounds and stored energy in our chakras, our business and our world comes back together.

When we hold onto hatred or resentment toward a coworker, former friend or spouse, or government official, it can indirectly cause hatred and resentment within other people and contribute to a culture of hate. Recent examples, such as the Me Too! Movement, Black Lives Matter, Conscious Capitalism, and similar movements, reflect the coming together of people with similar wounds and passions, knowing their collective power will change the world.

There are two important things to realize about your chakras and your business:

1. *Stuck energy from past failures, tragedies, and disappointments will hold you back.* It may not be tangible, but this energy will keep you from being as successful as you can be in your business. You cannot separate your personal life from your business success.

2. *Clearing that stuck energy will unleash the energy that leads to success.* You will be able to make a much bigger difference in the world when you are fully aligned within your own energy centers and on purpose, especially when you tie that to ingredients three and four below.

Just as each chakra is tied to specific life areas and issues, each chakra also represents a different stage of developing and growing your business. In Parts 2 through 5, we will explore in detail specific wounds tied to each of the chakras, as well as the business tasks that must be mastered in order to complete the work required by that vibration and energy. We will also provide you with a chakra clearing meditation for each of the chakras as we explore them.

3. HOW TO USE THE CREATION LAWS IN YOUR BUSINESS

So now you know you have an inner energy roadmap within your chakras that guides you to experience what you want or the lack thereof. Another invisible tool you have to use in incorporating Conscious Client Attraction into your business is the Creation Laws.

The majority of entrepreneurs develop their strategy, branding, marketing and sales approach based solely on what can be measured, seen, and perceived with the physical senses. They look to the numbers as their only gauge of success.

What these entrepreneurs fail to realize is that they are manifesting their results unconsciously because they are unaware of the Creation Laws. Every single person on the planet is manifesting right now, whether they realize it or not. You can either create your results consciously or unconsciously – by default – and once you are aware and can consciously direct the Creation Laws, they can absolutely catapult your success.

No doubt you have heard of the Law of Attraction, popularized in recent years by the movie "The Secret." But it has been around long before that – along with other Creation Laws, such as the Law of Guidance, the Law of Alignment, the Law of Specificity, and more. There is one primary Law related to each of the eight phases of Conscious Client Attraction.

While there are many different components that comprise the Conscious Client Attraction system, when it comes to attracting clients, the energy of your communication is critical. Experts tell us that at least

57 percent of communication is non-verbal – in that is not just about body language and tone of voice! It also pertains to whether or not you are aligned with what you are selling, whether are not you feel desperate for money today, and whether you are coming from a genuine attitude of service or not.

What the Creation Laws allow us to do is accelerate the results we obtain in business, as well as in life. We can jump levels, as Price Pritchett writes in *You²*, and realize exponential improvement in our results, while actually taking *less* action in the physical world. This quantum physics principle can open your mind to all kinds of potential results and pathways that your logical mind could not conceive.

Perhaps you can now see that building a successful business as a Conscious Expert is about much more than just putting words to paper or having a snazzy website. It is about sharing your unique gifts, doing the work on yourself to clear your chakras, using the Creation Laws consciously, and having a solid strategy. It may feel like a bit of a Rubik's cube right now, but if you will stay with me and apply what we explore together step-by-step, you will be able to create a business beyond your wildest dreams.

4. THE CONSCIOUS BUSINESS STRATEGY

I expect many of you reading this book have some grasp of business strategy and a basic knowledge about packaging your services, marketing, selling, and the like. So the first three ingredients above may be the primary aha's for you. However, even if you know business strategy, what is different about our eight-part Client Attraction Blueprint presented here is that it seamlessly integrates the invisible elements we have just discussed with a step-by-step approach that I and my clients have used successfully to generate millions of dollars.

Other readers may be very comfortable with the idea of one's calling, the chakras, and the Creation Laws – but have no idea how to leverage and monetize the spiritual gifts they have through a proven business strategy. They fear that they may feel too constrained by creating structure around their inner world. And yet, that may be the exact life lesson they are now to learn now: how to express their spiritual nature and gifts within a container that generates money.

In my experience, spiritually based entrepreneurs tend to shy away from earning money – which is usually a chakra wound in itself – for fear that it will contaminate their gifts somehow. But spirituality and wealth are not incompatible. In fact, spiritual icons such as Mother Teresa, Gandhi, and others always had plenty of money provided to them through the work they did. Remember, the more money you earn, the more people you can help.

We will be exploring each of these eight key steps in building a consciously based business over the course of the rest of the book. But just to show you a sneak peek of what we will be creating together, see Fig. 6, which illustrates the phases in our Conscious Business Strategy – known as the Conscious Client Attraction Blueprint.

FIG. 6 THE CONSCIOUS CLIENT ATTRACTION BLUEPRINT

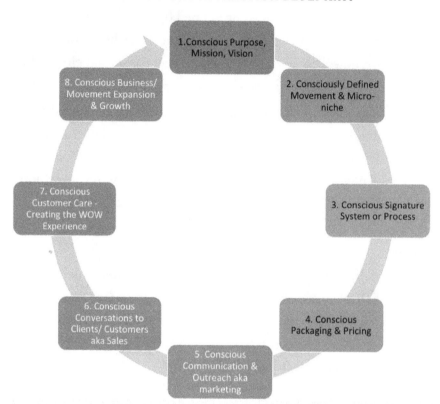

THE 8 CHAKRA BUSINESS TYPES

As you will see during our journey, the concept for the type of business you launch and grow – as well as the people you serve – usually emerges from your triumph over a tragedy or tough situation. That challenge is tied to one of your eight chakras – and in turn, your business helps your Tribe heal that chakra.

We call these the 8 Chakra Business Types. They are summarized here and discussed in more detail in each chapter that explores the individual chakras.

Chakra Business Type 1, Grounding, is a business that helps people reconnect to their essential self, their family and their tribe and feel secure. It may also help people clarify their life purpose and remain grounded despite challenges.

Chakra Business Type 2, Expressive, is a business that helps people express their creativity and their sexuality or intimate connections with others. It may also help people tame their appetites (e.g., weight loss or addiction treatment).

Chakra Business Type 3, Empowerment, is a business that helps people step into their personal power, which may involve overcoming fear, small thinking and shame. It may also help people shift from attempting to control outside circumstances to expanding their vibration to fully serve.

Chakra Business Type 4, Lover, is a business that helps people embrace love – self-love, love for one's intimate partner, or universal love for all of humanity. It may also help people express love in the form of charging what they are worth, finding their mate, or attracting their ideal tribe in a compassionate way.

Chakra Business Type 5, Teacher, is a business that helps people speak their truth – whether that is in their family relationships, in their job, or in their business. It may also help people overcome shyness or introversion, anxiety or physical throat problems that have an energetic base.

Chakra Business Type 6, Intuitive, is a business that helps people access their intuition and spiritual gifts (clairvoyance, clairaudience, healing gifts, etc.). It may also help people overcome repression of their intuition, creativity and imagination from childhood.

Chakra Business Type 7, Connector, is a business that helps people connect more deeply to their concept of God, the Universe or the Divine. It may also help people heal religious wounds from childhood, as well as anger or resentment toward God or feelings of separation stemming from a past tragedy.

Chakra Business Type 8, Oneness, is a business that helps people embody oneness with humanity, God and creation. It may also help people heal wounds at other chakras that cause disruption in their aura.

Let's get started with chakra 1 and secret 1!

PART 2

IDENTIFYING YOUR CALLING AND MAGNETIC MOVEMENT

CHAPTER 3

SECRET # 1: YOUR CONSCIOUS PURPOSE, MISSION, AND VISION

"When I was two years old, my family home caught fire. Not only was it destroyed – but also my father and two sisters were killed. I don't know how long I lived in the hospital with third degree burns on my face, chest, arms and legs. When I finally returned home, my mother was a changed woman. I can't explain how lonely I felt. Her drinking problem became apparent in just a few years. She remarried when I was four and had my sister, Brenda, when I was seven. Then, my stepdad was killed in a logging accident when my sister was two. Mom remarried, this time to a man with a serious drinking problem. When I was 25, my mom and stepdad bought a neighborhood bar, in which she was shot and killed in a robbery two months later.

"As you can imagine, these early life events led to an ongoing sense of uncertainty, fear, and low self-esteem that took me years to regain – if I ever had them at all! I desperately tried to find it in dysfunctional relationships, and comforted myself with shopping, promiscuity, overeating and working. Still I was left feeling empty. Even becoming a special education teacher and a counselor, getting a doctorate degree, and later becoming a university professor did little to truly rebuild my self-esteem.

"I began to find peace by learning and practicing a variety of healing techniques and delving deep into my spiritual practice. In 2008, I started my own business as a healer. It wasn't until I discovered a healing technique that totally resonated with me, and began applying it to myself, that I released much of the emotional pain in my life. I came to feel I mattered."

— *Dr. Lynne Cockrum-Murphy, Healer*

Since this traumatic event happened so early in Lynne's life, it shook her to the core. As she explored both ineffective strategies as well as solutions that worked, she began doing personal healing work and finally felt grounded once again.

WHAT YOU'LL LEARN IN THIS CHAPTER

- Chakra 1 and Its Impact
- The Chakra 1 Business Type
- The Creation Law of Purpose
- How to Discover Your Life's Purpose
- How to Express Your Business Mission
- How to Create Your Vision
- How to Choose Your Business Model
- Legal, Financial and Office Setup Logistics

CHAKRA 1: BASE/ROOT CHAKRA

WHAT THE BASE CHAKRA FOCUSES ON

The base chakra is located at the base of your spine, in your tailbone area. And just as you rely on your spine to support you when walking or sitting or standing, the base chakra supports and grounds you in every aspect of your life.

It is what gives you that sense of safety, security, and stability. It is also what provides your sense of belonging, both to your family unit and to your culture, tribe and race.

When this energy center is healthy, you'll feel like your life is on a solid footing and that nothing can shake your confidence.

Your business's purpose, mission and vision will provide the same kind of stability and unshakable commitment that a healthy base chakra does in the individual.

HOW TO KNOW IF THE 1ST CHAKRA IS BLOCKED

At a personal level, you will know that your first chakra is blocked if you feel anxious, afraid, different, or simply scattered in your focus. You may be suspicious, especially when it comes to investing your money or accepting other people's help. Whatever initially wounded that chakra causes a knee-jerk reaction of wanting to stay safe – which makes you risk-averse as well.

In the business setting, you may have trouble determining exactly what kind of business you want to start. And when you do start moving in one direction, you second-guess yourself. You might start one business after another, try network marketing or some other kind of opportunity for a while, but feel like you can't get off the starting blocks.

If you have an existing business, your staff will feel confused, fragmented, and overwhelmed because they don't have a sense of a bigger purpose, overall direction or meaning in their work.

Morale, even if it was once high, declines - and with that sales decline. You know you haven't reviewed the company's vision in a year or more - and/or no one knows what it is.

And believe it or not, a significant wound at that fundamental level of energy in your personal life could have the ripple effect of an ongoing lack of vision and willingness to take risks when you become an entrepreneur.

WOUNDS THAT CAN BLOCK CHAKRA 1

So what kinds of wounds cause the base chakra to get out of alignment? Being adopted, especially within the first few days or months of life, can cause a base chakra wound, because at a deep (often unconscious) level, you feel like you aren't wanted.

Losing a parent can also cause a base chakra wound. One out of every seven people in the U.S. loses a parent before the age of 20. I am no exception – my father died when I was 13. It is worth noting that the majority of female entrepreneurs have an absent father during childhood, whether due to addiction, emotional distance, death, or divorce.

Divorce, abuse, growing up in financial poverty or near poverty, as well as any experiences of abandonment by those significant to you, can wound your sense of safety and security.

THE CHAKRA 1 BUSINESS TYPE

Chakra Business Type 1, Grounding, is a business that helps people reconnect to their essential self, their family and their tribe and feel secure. It may also help people clarify their life purpose and remain grounded despite challenges.

Examples include some healers, rebirthing specialists, life coaches, family relationship coaches, life purpose coaches and the like.

CHAKRA 1 CLEARING & ACTIVATION

See marciabench.com/cca-book-resources for the clearing and activation process for Chakra 1.

CHAKRA 1 CREATION LAW: THE LAW OF PURPOSE

The Law of Purpose simply states that without direction, there is no manifestation. Everything has a purpose, including you, each of the people in your life, and even the fact you are reading this book right now.

You make decisions every day about where and how you work, with whom you get into relationship, and many smaller choices. The more you can make these choices based on intention and purpose, instead of logic or random chance, the more you will align with the Law of Purpose.

BUSINESS TASKS ASSOCIATED WITH CHAKRA 1

So what business tasks correlate with the base chakra? They include:

- How to Discover Your Life's Purpose
- How to Express Your Business Mission
- How to Create Your Vision
- How to Choose Your Business Model
- Legal, Financial and Office Setup Logistics

Let's discuss each in turn.

HOW TO DISCOVER YOUR LIFE'S PURPOSE

For life and our work to have meaning, we must know our life's purpose, our calling and our Tribe (who we are meant to serve). Life purpose is the filter for our choices.

WHAT LIFE PURPOSE IS

What is encompassed by the term *life purpose?* First, in a broad sense, we all have a shared overall purpose, in that we are here to discover as much of our true self as we can, and to express it through our life. We do this through all the experiences we have, the people we relate to, the jobs we choose, and the teachers, coaches, and mentors, whose message rings true for us. But that is not our primary emphasis here.

Each of us also has a specific life purpose. It is a calling, a mission, or an overall theme for our life that transcends our daily activities. It is the quality we are here on earth to develop, the type of service we are to render, the way we can enhance or improve some segment of the planet. And ultimately, our business is a vehicle through which we express our purpose.

QUALITIES OF LIFE PURPOSE

Fulfilling one's life purpose is fun, joyful, satisfying and playful. When we are carrying out our life purpose, we find that time goes by unnoticed. Hours pass by in pure bliss and complete happiness. As a central theme for our life, our life purpose also helps us decide whether to accept a particular contract or client, whether to volunteer for a particular cause, and which kinds of relationships - professional and personal - will best contribute to fulfilling our purpose.

HOW TO DISCOVER YOUR LIFE PURPOSE

Some people find themselves exploring their life purpose early in life; others don't address it until midlife or beyond. And often, it is so obvious that it is right in front of us - and if we asked our best friends or family what our purpose is, they would be able to shed some light on it.

But ultimately, it needs to come from us.

Since the beginning, the work I have done as an entrepreneur has had its roots in life purpose. I spent 18 years – starting at the age of 14 – trying to figure out what mine was. Interestingly, my breakthrough happened after doing many exercises, attending many seminars, reading many books, and asking many experts. My Eureka moment was when I started my first business and finally had no limits on what I could do, whom I could serve, or what kind of income I could make.

Therefore, I developed tools from my own exploration process, and later from my work with thousands of entrepreneurs, to help people just like you discover your purpose.

The good news is, the shorter of the two tools is the most effective for entrepreneurs. It is a simple four-question formula, which even if you've been moving towards clarifying your purpose for years, often causes breakthroughs in 10 to 15 minutes.

The formula goes like this (see Fig. 7, Formula for Your Life's Purpose):

1. **What do you love to do?** List three to five favorite activities, whether they are related to work or what you enjoy doing in your spare time.

2. **What was your greatest emotional pain in childhood?** In other words, was there something that happened to you – like the fire that Lynne experienced (or something less dramatic) – that greatly influenced you and continues to do so now? Perhaps you had a series of experiences, such as sexual abuse on repeated occasions, or struggling to have enough food and clothing. List the first thing that comes to mind, whether it was in childhood or whether it was later in life, such as losing a child or having your spouse break up your marriage over an affair.

3. **What are your natural gifts and talents?** What are things you knew how to do, even before you did them? What are the aspects of your current work or hobbies that came easily to you? What would others say your greatest gifts are? Name three to five of these.

4. **Whom do you long to help?** If there were one group of people in the world with whom you can make a difference, who would they be? Try to be as specific as possible. Maybe it is female executives in the aerospace industry who are planning their retirement career, or college students who feel hopeless and are looking for direction, as two examples.

FIG. 7 - FORMULA FOR YOUR LIFE'S PURPOSE:

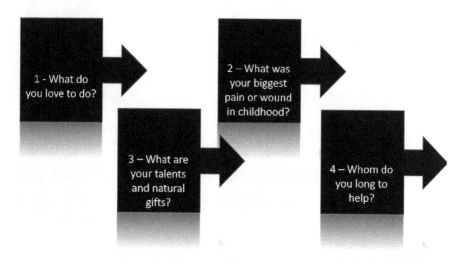

Now, put your answers to these four questions in sequence by filling in the blanks below:

My life's purpose is to use my love of [#1 – what I love] and my talents and gifts of [#3 – talents and natural gifts] to help [#4 – whom you long to help] overcome [#2 wound].

What did you discover?

It may seem a bit clunky and awkward in your initial draft, but my guess is that the essence of your purpose is there. And here's the bonus: this is also the essence of the work you are here to do. For example, here is my purpose statement using the formula:

"My life's purpose is to use my love of transformation and my talents and gifts of synthesizing information, creating systems, speaking, writing and coaching to help spiritually minded entrepreneurial experts overcome their lack of clarity and create a profitable business around their life purpose."

For a longer version of life purpose exploration, you can access the three-part audio series and worksheet called 10 Clues to Discovering Your

Life's Purpose, including my Symbol Meditation, at the book resources page here: marciabench.com/cca-book-resources.

HOW TO EXPRESS YOUR BUSINESS MISSION

Your business mission is the transformation or legacy it will leave behind, that is, how it will improve the world (or the segment of people that it serves). Although you and your business are connected energetically, your business is nevertheless a separate entity. Therefore, it needs to have its own mission statement to articulate what it is here to accomplish.

The mission of your business and the purpose of your life need to be aligned. Think of your life purpose as the umbrella over all aspects of your life. Your business, your relationships, your health, your leisure activities, and all other aspects of who you are fall within it. If any one of those elements is misaligned with your purpose, it will affect all of the others.

You will want to include four components in your business mission statement, as illustrated in Fig. 8:

First, what is the overall purpose of the business? You will usually state this as, "XYZ business's purpose is to help _____ do/accomplish/overcome _____ so they can _____ _____."

For example, my business' mission statement is:

"Marcia Bench Enterprises' mission is to help visionary coaches, healers, authors, speakers and other entrepreneur experts share their unique gifts with their ideal clients with joy, ease, and financial flow, so they can clearly identify, express, leverage and monetize their life purpose and be fulfilled."

Second, you will want to articulate the philosophy or values behind your business. Are there some basic tenets to which you subscribe? Are there certain values that are important for you to integrate into your operations?

Some of our philosophy was explained in the eight principles outlined in chapter 1. Key values include honoring the client as whole and complete, facilitating freedom and creative expression, holding our clients and ourselves accountable, integrating Creation Laws into business, and more.

The third element of your business mission statement is the key objectives or sub–purposes your business is here to fulfill. These can be key initiatives, an elaboration of some of the values in element two, or the avenues through which you serve your clients.

Some of our objectives would include transforming the success paradigm for entrepreneurs to incorporate spirituality, as well as strategy; creating world-class training and mentoring programs designed to help entrepreneurs excel; and expanding our online impact through a multi-channel presence.

Finally, your business mission statement should explain how it is congruent with the life purpose of the owner – you. This is not something you need to communicate to the public, but something you need to clarify internally.

For example, Marcia Bench Enterprises is the container and means through which I express my purpose of helping Conscious Experts live their life purpose fully through their business.

FIG. 8 - 4 COMPONENTS OF YOUR BUSINESS MISSION

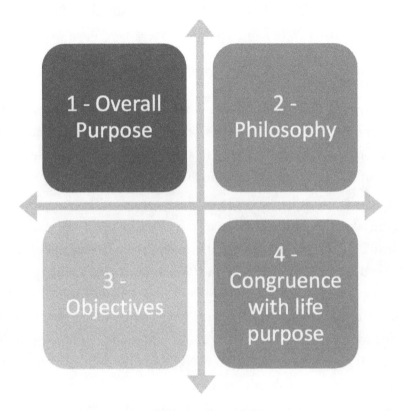

Use the Conscious Business Mission Statement worksheet at the book resources page here marciabench.com/cca-book-resources to craft yours.

HOW TO CREATE YOUR VISION

When I was still practicing law, I began doing seminars for employers periodically and teaching classes at a local community college. I discovered that I loved public speaking and wanted to do more of it to attract clients. But it seemed to be slow going, juggling my law practice and trying to speak as well. I kept thinking that over a period of time, my part-time consulting business would build up to where I would become known and hired as a speaker. I saw people like Dr. Wayne Dyer, Dr. Deepak Chopra, and the people in my local speakers association doing it – and I wanted it.

One weekend, I was at the Oregon coast and happened to see an infomercial with Tony Robbins. He asked a life-changing question, *"What if you could begin living your dream right now? What would be your first step?"*

It was as if the world stopped.

I discovered that I not only knew my first step, but I knew several of the other steps that would follow. I would write a book, sell my home, sell my law practice, buy an RV to live in and take my message to the people, instead of waiting for them to come to me.

My vision immediately began to come together. The very next week I began taking steps that I knew to take, and followed my guidance as to what I was to do next. Six months later, my book was published, my home and law practice were sold, the RV was purchased and the initial 10 bookings of what would become a ten-month, 65-city national speaking tour, via motor home, were booked. Even better, divine synchronicity had led me to contact Hay House about publishing my book, and they accepted it on the first inquiry. They accelerated the publication date after discovering that I was already on tour.

About a year later, at an event hosted by Hay House, I had the privilege of sharing the stage with Dr. Wayne Dyer, and found out that he too had sold everything after leaving his tenured college professorship and began traveling to do seminars around the country.

WHY HAVE A WRITTEN VISION?

Could some of those things have happened without me having a vision? Perhaps, but it would have been much more by chance than by choice.

I have used vision statements to create amazing opportunities for new jobs and careers, to find my soulmate, and to manifest clients, business opportunities, and money. Whenever I begin working with a new client, writing a vision statement is the first thing I have them do. It actually amazes me how few people know what they want out of life!

People frequently contact me wanting to hire me to coach them, and when I ask them what income they want to earn this year, what kind of clients they want to work with, and what other goals they have for their business, I hear silence. They do not know.

As you will see when we explore the Law of Attraction a little bit later, we can only manifest what we imagine. We can only imagine what we desire. And as Raymond Holliwell points out in his amazing book, *Working with the Law,* "No desire is felt until the supply is ready to appear."

When we look at the great thought leaders past and present, we see the power of vision. Martin Luther King, Jr. said, "I have a dream..."

Stephen Covey said, "Begin with the end in mind."

When a Harvard graduating class was studied over a 20-year period, only 3% of the graduates had a vision and a written plan for its achievement. That was surprising in itself, given the fact that they were high achievers who qualified to attend and complete their education at Harvard. But it the end of the 20 years, that 3% was worth more than the entire class put together and measured higher on scales for life satisfaction. Vision does make a difference.

The subconscious actually responds better to images than to words. John Assaraf, of the movie "The Secret," tells the story of creating a vision board with pictures of his ideal home, finances, relationships and the like – and then being called to move to another state for a business opportunity. He lived there for five years. In moving back to San Diego, five years later, his son happened to open the box that had his vision board in it. He asked his dad, "What's this, Dad?" John looked at it and his jaw literally dropped. The picture of the house on the vision board was the exact same one he had just moved into. Not one like it - but the exact same one, from a picture he had taken out of a magazine five years prior, not knowing how literally the Universe would take his intention.

ELEMENTS OF SUCCESSFUL VISION

In order to create a successful vision statement, it needs to satisfy six key elements, as illustrated in Figure 9.

FIGURE 9 - ELEMENTS OF A SUCCESSFUL VISION STATEMENT

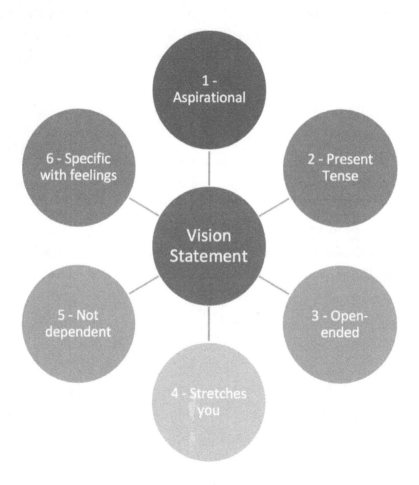

1. **Aspirational:** your vision statement should lift you up and inspire you. It should call forth a higher expression of who you are.

2. **Present tense:** your vision statement should be written in the present tense, i.e. "I am now…" not "I will" or "I want." You should be imagining yourself experiencing what you are saying as you say it.

3. **Open-ended:** your vision statement should be what Ernest Holmes calls, "open at the top," that is, it is not limited by what you can imagine. Include phrases like "this or something better" or "this much money or more" or "at least x number of new clients."

4. **Stretches you:** your vision statement should stretch you. If it didn't, it wouldn't be a vision statement - it would be your current reality. Just be sure you don't try to lose 100 pounds in one month or something unreasonable – make it a stretch, but not impossible.

5. **Not dependent on others:** your vision statement should not depend on others taking action in order for you to have it. For example, you might say that your vision is to have your boss's job, but that would depend on the boss leaving the job. Ask yourself what it is about having that position which represents your true desire – whether it is more responsibility, more challenge, more freedom, or more pay – and state that as your vision.

6. **Specific with feelings:** your vision statement should be specific enough that you can recognize and measure it so you know it has happened. Having a vision that your spouse will be more loving toward you may mean something different to you than it does to him/her. Be sure to include the emotions that you expect to feel when your vision is realized – as though you are experiencing it right now. Then, make the choice to start having the feeling, even before you have the manifestation. That will speed things up for you.

Use the Business & Life Vision worksheet on the book resources page at marciabench.com/cca-book-resources to craft yours for the next six months, one year and three years.

HOW TO CHOOSE YOUR BUSINESS MODEL

Now you know your life purpose, your business mission, and your vision for the next six months, the next year and next three years. Those are key steps that many entrepreneurs simply skip.

The final step in this building process is to choose one of the five most commonly used Conscious Expert business models, as illustrated in Fig. 10, to help you achieve your purpose, mission and vision. I have used all of these models in various stages in my business, and have helped clients implement them as appropriate.

FIG. 10 - 5 COMMON CONSCIOUS EXPERT BUSINESS MODELS

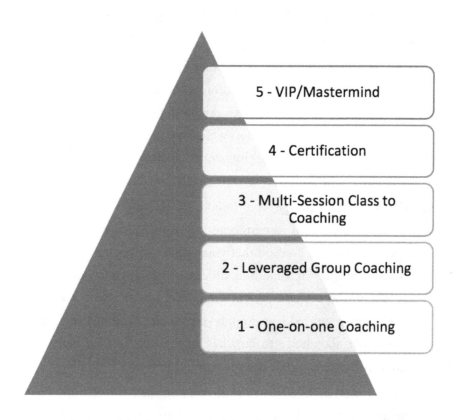

Your choice of the business model will depend on several factors:

- Whether you are a start-up or an established business.
- Whether you enjoy a primarily one-on-one service model or wish to leverage your service delivery.
- Whether you enjoy facilitating online groups or not.
- Whether you have a proven Conscious Signature System or not.

- How big your vision is and how many people you want to serve.

Here is a brief summary of the five business models. (Note: if you are an author or have other information products, you would either use these models as an upsell from the initial product purchase, or you would embed your products within your chosen business model as bonuses to enhance information transfer.)

1. ONE-ON-ONE COACHING MODEL

In this model, just as it sounds, you work with your clients one-on-one. I am highly partial to virtual coaching over a conference line, as opposed to face-to-face coaching to simplify the logistics, but it can be done either way.

Of course, your clients love this because they get a lot of time with you. This is the model most coaches, healers, nutritionists and similar experts start with, because it allows you to test your service delivery model, to make adjustments along the way, and to choose the number of people with whom you will work.

However, it is extremely labor-intensive and hard to scale. If your vision is to start a global movement and create a massive change within your select market, individual coaching will only be sustainable for a short time. And if, like many of my clients, you start attracting so many leads that you cannot serve them all as individual clients, you will have to move into one of the other four models.

2. LEVERAGED GROUP COACHING MODEL

In this model, you design one or more levels of a group coaching/training program designed to serve your clients with common needs. In the early days of the coaching industry, group coaching was seen as something you provided for those could not afford individual coaching. That is no longer the case.

In fact, having participated in several of these programs as a client, I actually believe they offer greater value than the individual coaching alone. Group members often connect with each other and provide additional support when you are not available. I particularly like these groups for entrepreneurs because co–participants in the group can support each other's work as joint venture partners when their interests are aligned, but not identical.

Normally, you would only choose the group delivery model once you have tested your Conscious Signature System (see next chapter) of steps you use in working with individual clients.

Example: One of my clients, Melissa, enthusiastically enrolled as many as 14 new individual clients per month for several months, until she finally realized that she couldn't keep offering her services that way. There just aren't enough hours in the day. So she created a group program to avoid having to turn clients away, due to lack of time.

Typically, group coaching programs are a combination of training and coaching. The training can be live or pre-recorded, and live sessions offered weekly or every other week, via conference line, in which participants ask questions around that week's topic. They typically last for three to six months or even up to a year. You can offer two levels, one that only includes the training and the live group calls, and another that includes the group training/coaching plus individual sessions one or two times per month.

One of the big advantages of group programs is that your clients tend to be more committed in these programs because they have invested in a longer-term solution. You get to spend less time serving more clients, while scaling your numbers, and only coach individually with those who are willing to invest at a higher level. And the laser coaching that happens on the live calls is done with one individual at a time, so they are still getting customized support.

There really is no disadvantage to this model, other than the need to have a strategy to fill it. You will either embrace the Launch Model (see chapter 7) and open the program for new members at certain intervals, or use the Rolling Enrollment Model that yields an ongoing supply of qualified leads to join the group along the way.

3. MULTI-SESSION CLASS TO COACHING MODEL

In this model, you extract the common steps and techniques that you've been using in your individual services, and teach those steps as a multi-week webinar series or weekend workshop. For example, if there are six key steps for your clients to move from their pain, to their desired outcome, you would create a class lasting six weeks, promote it and teach it.

Toward the end of the course, you offer a discount, a bonus or another incentive to work with you personally as a client, either individually or in a structured group implementation program, lasting three to six months after the class.

The biggest advantage of this model is that it is usually easier to sell a class than it is individual coaching. During the class, the students get to know you and your approach, and many will want help in implementing what you have taught them. That is exactly how my first consulting client came about.

Your time commitment is less than either model 2 or 3. Although you would charge less per person for the class than you would for a coaching package, you would make many times that with upsells to follow-up coaching. You're also able to serve a greater number of people in less time, so your impact is greater. And promoting the class builds brand awareness as well.

4. CERTIFICATION MODEL

A fourth model for delivering your services is the certification model. People in virtually any services industry, as well as any authors of books that outline a particular system for change (weight loss, healing, marketing, social media, business start-up, coaching, etc.), can use this model. The primary prerequisite is that you must have a solid Conscious Signature System (series of steps people need to take in order to achieve the end result with which you help them).

In 2001, after 15 years as an entrepreneur and several years helping people with career development needs, I launched the certification business model to literally invent the industry of career coaching. I founded my company, Career Coach Institute, after I completed my basic and master level coaching credentials. I then combined coaching techniques and the proven career development model that I had used with my private clients to form the certification. I had also tested the model in weekend workshops and classes.

What I quickly discovered, and continue to be amazed by, is that the certification model is one of the easiest to sell. People are seeking mastery and ongoing continuing education, especially if they see that by completing your certification, they can start a new business, new career, or otherwise share their transformation with others. We deliver our certification online, which makes it all the more convenient for us and for our busy students. Graduates of the certification program become candidates for our Conscious Client Attraction business coaching as well.

This is a business model that can allow you to put a portion of your business on autopilot. Most certification providers require monthly or annual fees, license fees to use their content, or other continuing education in order to create ongoing revenue streams. Requiring fees for renewal of the credential, dues for membership in your professional association, or tickets for attending certain events you sponsor can also be added.

The only branding issue you will need to think through before offering certification is whether or not having others certified to do what you do will dilute your brand or strengthen it.

5. VIP/MASTERMIND MODEL

The fifth and final model for expert services delivery is the VIP/mastermind model. It has some of the elements of group coaching in it, but is offered as an elite program, typically involving quarterly retreats for the group, often in person.

The typical mastermind program lasts at least six months, and most last a full year. Each month your clients will receive content in the form of a live or prerecorded training – or more than one. And either as a part of those training calls or separately, they will get the chance to participate in private question-and-answer/laser coaching calls weekly or twice per month.

Most Mastermind programs have two levels. For example, the lower level could include group coaching and training only, and the higher level would add two individual sessions per month with you or one of your other professionals. Also, one level could include a half-day VIP day 1:1 with you, either over conference line or in person, where you provide intensive individualized guidance to them. One or both levels can include the quarterly retreats.

The Mastermind model is the most lucrative of all the models, since the typical investment level is anywhere from $20,000 up to $100,000 for the year. It is the most leveraged and tends to attract the most highly committed clients.

Here again, you must have a solid Conscious Signature System for this to be successful. Each month of the program can be devoted to a separate element of your system, or you can organize it a different way. These programs are difficult to fill other than through a live two- or three-day event setting. Therefore, you would need to be up to the challenge of planning, filling, and hosting such an event, if you wish to have your own mastermind group.

LEGAL, FINANCIAL AND OFFICE SETUP LOGISTICS

In building your business foundation, I would be remiss if I did not mention the importance of making sure that your I's are dotted and T's are crossed on the legal and financial end of things.

Legally, you need to choose whether or not to incorporate or be a Limited Liability Company ("LLC"), have the contracts that you're using with clients reviewed by a lawyer in your jurisdiction before you use them, protect your intellectual property, and be sure that your relationships with any virtual or in-person staff are handled properly. I highly recommend Legal Shield as an affordable way to get the counsel you need. See the book resource list at marciabench.com/cca-book-resources for more information.

Financially, from the very beginning you need to list your start-up investments, track your business income and expenses, and mind your taxes as a self-employed business owner. There are some very expensive "lessons" you will need to learn if you do not get counsel up front on these issues. One of my clients took a loan against their retirement plan to pay for extensive start-up expenses, and found they had a huge tax bill the next year as a result. They also paid double tax on their income because they did not choose the right legal entity for their business.

I recommend that you talk to fellow business owners in your area in order to get the name of a good CPA who is also familiar with small-business taxation. In addition, you'll ultimately need a bookkeeper, once you begin earning money. In the meantime, be sure to review the IRS publication, *Tax Guide for Small Businesses,* to get a better idea of what is deductible and what is not on your taxes.

Please consult the book resource page at marciabench.com/cca-book-resources for our Four-Month Business Start-up Checklist make sure you have covered all your bases.

CHAPTER 4

SECRET # 2: YOUR MAGNETIC MOVEMENT & MICRO-NICHE

"Born with a disability in my eyes, I learned how to overcome adversity and stereotyping. I developed a keen sense of self-awareness at an early age. My passion to see others discover freedom mentally, emotionally and spiritually became my life purpose. I experienced a deeper level of self-discovery during my own personal transformation, while studying for first coaching certification in 2007. Unbeknownst to me, this along with my faith, was what kept me going when illness began to consume my life in 2010.

"Migraines and severe back pain, mixed with abdominal pain, increased throughout the pregnancy of my second child. After my cholecystectomy (gall bladder removal surgery) in 2011, my health completely revolted and seizures riddled my frame of just under 5'9" and 106 pounds. After two years of ambulance rides, specialists, specialty clinics and a myriad of tests, scans and procedures, I was diagnosed with an incurable illness called Gastroparesis (paralysis of the stomach muscles). I could no longer consume food as an average person would. One of the top clinics in America placed me on a liquid to soft food diet, and sent me on my way. I was hospitalized four times for almost a week at a time. Every time they told me that if I didn't 'learn how to manage this disease,' hospital life would be my daily reality.

"I joined a few online support groups to learn about this illness, and found like-minded individuals who understood my plight. I began sending cards filled with glitter to lift their spirits, and they became quite popular. I then added monthly positivity challenges to reframe the patient's mindset away from the daily burden of living with chronic and debilitating conditions. Everything effortlessly expanded from there. I became a patient advocate. Members within our community began to volunteer in assisting me with my passion to make an impact in the lives of others, and I decided to form a non-profit organization as a disabled woman, affectionately known as Glitter Queens Global.

"This movement evolved, and through my work with Marcia and a challenge to create a signature system, my team and I created a new program that we will launch this year. It is one of the first online coaching programs for those battling chronic conditions of all kinds, entitled 'Chronically Well.' Within the first few social media announcements of our beta program, we had over 75 intended participants ready and waiting to enroll. My own book by the same name was just published. All of the above have been accomplished, in spite of being diagnosed and living every day with a chronic and incurable illness. I have spent countless hours in and out of physicians' offices, received nerve blocks, RFA's, and trigger point injections, all while maintaining the needs of a non-profit and that of a child with special needs."

— Coach April

April is a wonderful example of triumphing to share her gifts and help others heal and transform – despite significant physical limitations and setbacks tied to her second chakra, which encompasses the digestive system.

WHAT YOU'LL LEARN IN THIS CHAPTER
- Chakra 2 and Its Impact

- The Chakra 2 Business Type
- The Creation Law of Specificity
- How to Define Your Micro-Niche
- How to Identify the Problem You Solve
- How to Define Your Tribe
- How Your Brand Personality Affects Your Message and Niche
- What Your Transformational Story Is – and How to Use It

CHAKRA 2: SACRAL

WHAT THE SACRAL CHAKRA FOCUSES ON

The sacral chakra is located four inches above the base of your spine, in your stomach area. Situated at the part of the body where we digest our food, this chakra relates to appetites of various kinds, as well as the three aspects of creativity, sexuality and money.

It is what gives you the freedom to express yourself in all dimensions. Money, after all, is neutral in and of itself – it is simply a result or side effect of clear expression through creativity, authenticity and sexuality.

When this energy center is healthy, you'll feel like you can be and do what you naturally are – and your partner, your business Tribe, and others lovingly welcome it.

Your unique Micro-niche and Brand Personality – combined with your Conscious Signature System – form a unique identity for your business. In a healthy business, this message is communicated to its Tribe without impediment, and the Tribe happily responds.

HOW TO KNOW IF YOUR 2ND CHAKRA IS BLOCKED

Do you feel like your creativity is blocked, and everything feels like "same old, same old" with no innovation or newness? Or do you find yourself caught in addictive behaviors around food, alcohol, drugs, cigarettes or even chocolate? Is your sex life unsatisfying – or even nonexistent? And finally, are you constantly facing money difficulties, with "too much month at the end of the money?"

You may not think these issues are related – but they are! They are often centered on the sacral chakra. Opening the chakra in one aspect can open the others too – it can be amazing!

For example, my client Mary had a pattern of money shortage, going on for months, and just couldn't seem to get her coaching business off the ground. So I started asking her (tactfully of course, since I'm primarily a business coach, not a relationship coach!) how her marriage was. And she said there was distance between her and her partner, and they hadn't been intimate for months.

She shared that they used to love to dance, but hadn't done that for a long time. So I asked if she would be willing to go dancing with her spouse a couple of times before we met again and see how that impacted the relationship. She was skeptical, but agreed.

When she returned to the following week's session, she was beaming. Not only was the intimacy and joy back in her relationship with her husband – but she had had an income influx too!

We often think we can compartmentalize our lives so that an imbalance or lack of alignment in one area won't affect the rest – but we can't hide. All aspects of our lives are connected.

WOUNDS THAT CAN BLOCK CHAKRA 2

So what kinds of wounds cause the sacral chakra to get out of alignment?

These wounds can include sexual abuse, having your creative projects or ideas ridiculed, being parented with very strict rules, or being forced to suppress your true emotions in childhood.

Poverty and poverty-based thinking or training around money in childhood can affect not only the first, but the second chakra too.

THE CHAKRA 2 BUSINESS TYPE

Chakra Business Type 2, Expressive, is a business that helps people express their creativity and their sexuality or intimate connections with others. It may also help people tame their appetites (e.g., weight loss or addiction treatment).

Examples include couples coaches, sex therapists, creativity speakers and coaches, weight loss coaches and addiction experts and treatment centers, and some financial coaches and related services.

CHAKRA 2 CLEARING & ACTIVATION

See marciabench.com/cca-book-resources for Chakra 2 Clearing & Activation meditation.

CHAKRA 2 CREATION LAW: THE LAW OF SPECIFICITY

The Law of Specificity says that in order to manifest what you desire, you must state it specifically. It's the difference between saying you intend to attract more money, versus stating a specific minimum amount. It's the difference between saying you want more love in your life, versus specifying whether you want it to come from a new pet or a marriage partner.

You will remember our discussion in the last chapter that your vision should be specific, but also open at the top and not restricted to a particular form. In other words, you don't want to be overly specific, but you do need to be able to identify your desire once it has manifested.

The other principle at work with the Law of Specificity is that once you choose an intention, stay with it. Don't keep changing your mind and wonder why it isn't manifesting.

BUSINESS TASKS ASSOCIATED WITH CHAKRA 2

The business tasks that correlate with the sacral chakra include…

- How to Define Your Micro-Niche

- How to Identify the Problem You Solve
- How to Define Your Tribe
- How Your Brand Personality Affects Your Message and Niche
- What Your Transformational Story Is – and How to Use It

Let's discuss each one in depth.

HOW TO DEFINE YOUR MICRO-NICHE

A decade or two ago – before the proliferation of online businesses and the Internet – it was sufficient to have a fairly general description of what you do or sell, and begin blanketing your chosen market with invitations to buy it. The marketplace was not as complex as it is today, there were not as many choices, and the client or customer did not get overwhelmed so easily.

That has all changed now.

Just as online learning has evolved into providing micro–learning modules, niching has evolved into micro-niching, especially if you do business online as every business should be doing today.

There are at least five reasons to significantly narrow the scope of your market into a micro-niche today.

1. **General offerings don't work today.** Making the same general type of offer that you did 10 or 20 years ago – even if the other providers in your market are still doing so – will not resonate with your ideal clients today. They are seeking a way to sift and sort through thousands of marketing messages they are bombarded with every single day through multiple media. One of the ways to stand out from the rest it is to be more specific. For example, instead of being a business coach, one might call themselves an online marketing coach, or more specifically, a coach who helps entrepreneurs develop their lead magnet.

2. **Your Tribe will relate to you.** As you will see in a moment, we call the segment of the population that you are meant to serve your Tribe. These are people who are going through something you have already mastered, and they are seeking a solution. They will not only come to believe that you have the solution, but that you are the perfect person to provide it. Micro-niching is part of the secret to having that connection occur.

3. **You can turn your Micro-niche into a loyal Tribe and growing revenues.** Once you and your Tribe members have connected and they partake in your services, inevitably many of them will want more. So if they take a class from you, they may want to get customized coaching next, or to attend your next workshop or retreat. This doesn't happen when you have a diverse group of clients that do not share a common need and challenge. Once they do, they cling together - both to each other and to you - like survivors of a shipwreck, which leads to a growing business.

4. **Narrowing your focus in today's crowded marketplace is a survival strategy.** The future of the expert industry – particularly online – will require more specialization, not less. If you do not narrow your focus now, and continue to do so in the future, you will be left behind. Your business will not survive.

5. **Micro-niching is the only way to create a clear and lasting legacy and get people to seek you out.** In order to stop the dynamic of you chasing prospective clients to work with you - and instead, irresistibly attract them to you - you must stand for something. They must connect in their mind your name, mission and micro niche. Large companies have done this – when you think of FedEx, you think of overnight delivery. When you think of Richard Branson, you think of luxury and adventure. When you think of Google, you connect it with online search. Once you have defined

your Micro-niche, your Tribe will connect you with what you offer just as clearly.

NICHE VERSUS MICRO-NICHE

So what exactly are we referring to when we use the term Micro-niche?

First, let's define its ancestor, the niche. A "niche" refers to the general focus of what you do – e.g. job title "career coach" or "speaker" – combined with a general audience description.

A "Micro-niche," by contrast, answers four specific questions.

1. What **challenge or problem** do you help solve?
2. What specific **Tribe or "slice" of the market** do you serve?
3. What is your **Brand Personality** and how do you express it?
4. How does **your transformational story** provide meaning to the message?

1. HOW TO IDENTIFY THE PROBLEM YOU SOLVE

Think for a moment about why you started - or want to start - your Conscious Expert business. Nine times out of ten, it is because you have found a solution to a life issue, a business issue, a health issue, or something else with great meaning to you that motivates you to become a coach, author or other expert.

To identify the specific challenge or problem that you help, or want to help people solve, ask yourself these questions:

- What specifically do you want to help people become, accomplish, or achieve?
- How do you want to make the world a better place?
- If you are already offering professional or transformational services, which one component of what you do is the one that is most satisfying to you?
- In what area are you a genius at helping people?

You may want to look back at some of your answers to the Life Purpose exercise in chapter 3 to help you.

Also consider these questions, putting yourself in the mind and heart of your prospective clients:

- What problem keeps your prospects awake at night trying to find a solution?
- What current challenge or problem are your prospects confronting in their life that you're confident you could help them solve?
- What new technology, trend, regulation, or other development is on the horizon for your prospects that you could help them address now?

With the answers to these questions, you should be able to clearly finish the sentence, "I help my clients _____."

Here are a few examples…

- I help my clients find a new job quickly in the non-profit sector.
- I help my clients find ways to reverse their cancer without using traditional Western medicine.
- I help my clients develop a powerful lead magnet that attracts their ideal clients to them online.
- I help my clients release excess weight easily without having to diet.

2. HOW TO DEFINE YOUR TRIBE

After honing in on the specific challenge or problem with which you help clients, the second step in creating your Micro–niche is to specifically define who will benefit most from that solution. Nearly always, these people will have many of the same characteristics as you. They find themselves in a situation that you were in yourself a few months or years ago.

Defining your Tribe in this way brings up a lot of fear in new entrepreneurs. Logic says that if you offer your services to a broader audience, there are more prospects, and therefore there will be more sales.

The opposite is true. The more you go deep ("an inch wide and a mile deep") in a specific direction, instead of staying at the surface level ("an inch deep in a mile wide") - trying to be everything to everyone - the more quickly you will be able to build your business.

Imagine you attended a meeting last week where you met someone who had just lost 50 pounds and looked very healthy and happy. As a result, you asked them how they did it, they shared their solution with you, and you then start the same eating regimen. Naturally, you will want to share this with others – it's human nature. Are you more likely to share your newfound solution with people across the country from you, people that you don't work with or see every day, or people in your immediate circle?

Hopefully you get my point. People spend time with others who are like them. When you create a narrowly defined Tribe and start the momentum of referrals and success stories with that Tribe, you get better qualified prospects, and more of them in less time.

Some of the criteria you will want to clarify when defining your Tribe include things like age, gender, religion, politics, values, and more. See full Micro-niche Definition Worksheet in the book resource area at marciabench.com/cca-book-resources for all of the criteria you need to consider.

The standard by which to measure your Tribe definition is this: *are you easily able to identify professional associations to which they belong, the channels on social and regular media they watch, and the experts/thought leaders in that niche?* If not, keep working.

COMPETITION OR "RELATED PROVIDERS"?

Whether you are creating your Micro–niche at the beginning of your business or rebranding to change focus, it is very common to worry about competition. After all, I said earlier that the market has become more complex and crowded than ever before.

However, there is another way to think about this that is more in sync with the Conscious Client Attraction approach.

The truth is, there is no competition for your life purpose and its expression in the world. But many people find their life purpose is much bigger than they alone could fulfill. Other people will be called to a similar purpose, expressing it in their unique way to their unique Tribe.

I like to think of this as multiple players playing in the same sandbox. The name that we use in the world of Conscious Client Attraction for competitors is "Related Providers." That is, when someone is seeking your services, they will likely consider services from others with similar qualifications, but different perspectives and personalities. These are Direct Related Providers.

In addition, they will notice people who provide a portion of what you do, but not everything you do, such as a resume writer providing resume services, but not helping with career direction as a career coach would. These we call Overlapping Related Providers.

Third, there will be people who offer what you do and more. For example, outplacement firms provide coaching, resume services, and job-search support, so they would be Multi-dimensional Related Providers for a career coach. The test is, *"Would a person in my target market or the general public view company x as being in the same or a similar business to mine?"* See Fig. 11 for an illustration of the three types of Related Providers.

FIG. 11 - YOUR RELATED PROVIDERS

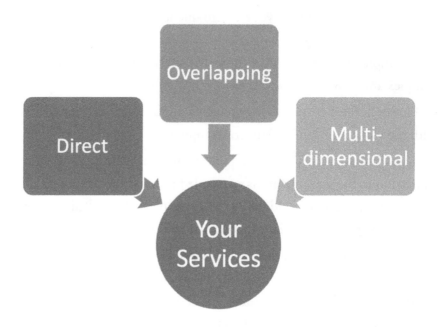

The fact is, even if someone else has the same degrees, certifications, and offerings that you do, your services are still unique because no one else is you. However, by establishing all four components of a Micro–niche, you help people distinguish you from the other Direct Related Providers – especially once you add your Brand Personality, the next component.

The reason you need to be aware of your Related Providers is not to depress you – though it might at first! It is easy to think others have already come up with the idea that you want to implement. But we advise that you become aware of who else is playing in your sandbox and compare them to the components and qualities you offer that make you unique. Beware if you come up with an idea and do not see any other Related Providers. Yes, you may have just come up with the greatest thing since sliced bread – but it may also be true that people have tried to launch in this niche and failed.

3. HOW YOUR BRAND PERSONALITY AFFECTS YOUR MESSAGE AND NICHE

The third aspect of your Micro–niche is your unique Brand Personality. A Brand Personality includes the particular meaning, visual representations, feelings, values and archetypes that you as the business owner bring to your brand. We mentioned FedEx above. Consider the difference in your perception of FedEx versus UPS. Even though both offer similar overnight delivery services, and neither is better or worse than the other. But you have a different perception of each based on their colors, their language, their logos, and the like.

Similarly, consider Starbucks versus Seattle's Best Coffee or Peet's Coffee. They all serve espresso, along with some pastry items, but each has a different way of expressing the values for which they stand.

Your Brand Personality affects everything in your business - from colors and fonts to images and language you use. It affects whom you attract, the price point you charge, how your offerings are perceived vis-à-vis others, and the inherent meaning of your brand to the public.

When the market was simpler a couple of decades ago, features of the product or service were the primary distinguishing factor between brands. When you went to choose a tube of toothpaste, you either picked Crest or Colgate – the choice was simple. When you went to choose which coffee shop to visit, it was strictly a function of what was convenient in your neighborhood. You didn't necessarily go out of your way to choose a specific type of coffeehouse, as people would do today with their favorite brand.

Now, by contrast, we have a whole section with multiple shelves and infinite variations of toothpaste to choose from, even between those two primary brands. So a new way to distinguish one brand from another has emerged. The way of distinguishing brands today is the meaning we find within a brand. We connect to that meaning so it becomes "our" brand, as Margaret Mark and Carol S. Pearson so artfully explain in *The Hero and the Outlaw*:

"The meaning of a brand is its most precious and irreplaceable asset... Meaning speaks to the feeling or intuitive side of the public; it creates an emotional affinity, allowing the more rational arguments to be heard."

Let me make this more practical. Imagine you go to the mall to shop at your favorite clothing store, and an outfit you absolutely love is on sale. You try it on, and think to yourself, "This would be perfect for my cousin's upcoming wedding. Look how it slims me in the right places, and it fits wonderfully. I think I would buy it even if it wasn't on sale." So you go ahead and purchase the outfit and take it home. Your spouse sees you carrying a bag and asks you about it. You explain that you found this great outfit – and saved hundred dollars on it. You probably don't say what you actually spent, but what you saved, right?

That is what the quote above refers to. You initially were drawn to the outfit on an emotional level, and fanned the flame of your connection to that outfit by how you thought about it and saw it fitting into your upcoming plans. The fact that it was on sale was a bonus – but when you explain it to your spouse, you focus on the logical, rational argument for how to justify the expense.

People do the same thing with our professional services. Of course, I don't want to suggest that you should encourage bargain hunters. But rather, if you will connect emotionally to your prospective clients first, and they know they are in the right place with the right person, the investment required to work with you will seem less important and easier to swallow. This is one of the reasons many Conscious Experts do not post their prices on their websites. They want to first establish the emotional connection before having the person disqualify themselves and lose interest, based only on what seems to be too high a price.

BRAND ARCHETYPES

One of the primary reasons you have a different experience with the various brands compared above is that they embrace different archetypes. In Jungian psychology, archetypes are defined as "a collectively inherited unconscious idea, pattern of thought, image, etc. universally present in individual psyches." There are 12 universally recognized archetypes that the subconscious recognizes and responds to. See Fig. 12 for the names of these archetypes.

FIG. 12 BRAND ARCHETYPES

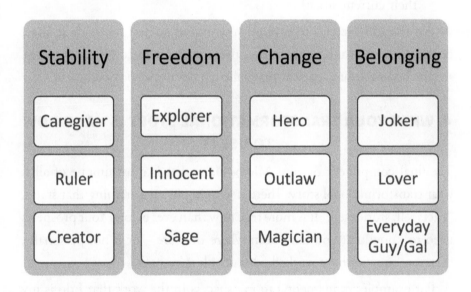

Your Brand Personality consists of a combination of the quirks, traits, and unique aspects of your human personality, combined with the archetypes expressed through your work in these three ways:

1. **For your services** – which of the archetypes best describes you and your approach to delivering your services?

2. **For your ideal clients** – which of the archetypes do your ideal clients /Tribe members relate to most?

3. **Where do 1 and 2 intersect?** – where is the intersection between what you want to deliver and the archetypes to which your clients are drawn? A common dilemma for Conscious Experts offering a transformational service is that they may relate more to change- or freedom-based archetypes, whereas the clients they attract are more drawn to and motivated by stability and belonging. Logo, colors, web design, and language must at the same time stimulate hope for a solution, while allowing the client to feel like you can relate to their current situation.

For the full exercise to explore your brand archetypes in these three categories, as well as how to connect the colors you use to your archetypes, see the book resource page at marciabench.com/cca-book-resources.

4. WHAT YOUR TRANSFORMATIONAL STORY IS – AND HOW TO USE IT

The final component of your Micro–niche that is most unique of all is your transformational story. There is a saying in sales training that states, "Facts tell, stories sell." It is more true now than ever before. Your prospects need to know that you have been where they are – or if not personally, that you know or have worked with people who have.

For example, fundamental to my success in the work that I do is my 18-year journey from feeling totally confused about why I was here, to knowing my life purpose with confidence and being able to help others discover theirs as well. My clients relate to my story of writing my first book in six months, selling my home and law practice and embarking on my first North American book/seminar tour by RV with only a few engagements on the calendar.

Your transformational story is "a pivotal life experience that influences you to such an extent that it causes you to want to help others overcome their situation or reach a similar goal." Remember the challenge or problem we talked about in factor one above? Here, we want to flesh out the experience or experiences you had that led you to be passionate about that challenge or problem.

I actually want you to write out a narrative story of the experience from the beginning – when you got the shocking diagnosis or noticed you were no longer happy with your work – all the way through to what you tried that didn't work, the solution you finally found, and the end results in detail.

Taking the time to do this now will make our next task much easier, which will involve culling out the key turning points in that story that will become your Conscious Signature System.

If you feel stuck or are not sure what your transformational story really is, create a timeline by decade with sticky notes on the wall or on a flipchart. Document the key emotionally charged, tragic, triumphant or transformational events that happened during each ten-year period. Then step back and notice any themes or any events that stand out from the rest.

What happened that:

- You are proud of?
- You were hurt by?
- You found difficult to get through?

That is your unique transformational story that will cause the rest of the elements of your Micro–niche to connect emotionally with your prospects.

In the case of April, whom we met at the opening of the chapter, her body made it clear what her transformational story was to be: overcoming pain and learning to live with the discomfort and dietary inconvenience of her chronic illness. It isn't always that obvious – but if you trust your intuition, then you will be guided to the story that you are meant to focus on in developing a solution that can help your clients.

PUTTING IT ALL TOGETHER

Now that you have clarified the challenge or problem you help people with, the exact Tribe of people that can benefit, your brand personality and your transformational story, you have the elements of a powerful Micro-niche. You can summarize it all as follows:

"I help _____[TRIBE]___ overcome/be/do _____ [CHALLENGE]_____ drawing on my Brand Personality Archetypes of _____, _____ and _____ and my story about _____."

Now, with this summary of your Micro-niche in hand, we are ready to turn it into a Conscious Signature System – and that is the focus of the next chapter.

PART 3

CREATING YOUR CONSCIOUS BRAND AND OFFER

CHAPTER 5

YOUR CONSCIOUS SIGNATURE SYSTEM

When she started her career coaching business, Melissa wasn't quite sure how to combine her decades as a recruiter with her newfound training through Career Coach Institute in career coaching. So she started out marketing to obtain clients to work one-on-one, with limited success.

She sat down and thought through what she'd learned about what makes candidates successful in getting the attention of recruiters and succeeding in the interview. She gathered a team, including resume writers, a resume distribution service, a Linkedin profile writer, a photographer and other specialists that she knew her clients would need.

Then she created her "Fast-Track To A New Job"™ – Proven Strategies "That Get Results!" program, using her proprietary "Reverse Job Search!"™ method. She began marketing herself through LinkedIn and live networking using this new system-based approach. The difference was staggering!

Her firm now offers one-on-one coaching, group coaching, and customized coaching packages to meet her clients' individual needs, using her Conscious Signature Systems designed for job seekers who want quick results. She enrolled 14 clients in just the first seven weeks, and nearly doubled that number in the next seven. Having a system instead of simply selling intangible career coaching services made all the difference.

WHAT YOU'LL LEARN IN THIS CHAPTER

- Chakra 3 and Its Impact
- The Chakra 3 Business Type
- The Creation Law of Alignment
- How to Create Your Conscious Signature System

CHAKRA 3: SOLAR PLEXUS

WHAT THE SOLAR PLEXUS CHAKRA FOCUSES ON

The solar plexus chakra is located right between your ribs, where your diaphragm is. Its primary focus is personal power and self-esteem, as well as taking responsibility for one's life and actions.

When it is healthy, you feel unstoppable – like you can do anything!

However, when it is blocked, you lack self-confidence, berate yourself, repel compliments, and may try to manipulate or control others to bolster your own visibility or achievements (usually unconsciously). You may find yourself playing the victim or reveling in having others take care of you - until something happens that motivates you to change. This is a key turning point in life and in business.

In your business, if your solar plexus is blocked, you will notice a compulsion to compare yourself with others in your field, and will experience sporadic income and high susceptibility to what is known as Bright Shiny Object Syndrome ("BSOS"). BSOS says, "buy this program/software/go to this event" and you will 'fix' what's wrong in your business." But if it stems from a blocked solar plexus chakra, no outside solution will fix the problem until you address the internal energy block or wound.

WOUNDS THAT CAN BLOCK CHAKRA 3

So what kinds of wounds cause the solar plexus chakra to get out of alignment?

If you have ever been told to sit down and shut up, or that good girls/boys should be seen and not heard, this is the type of cultural programming that can block the solar plexus. Being discounted or put down by parents, teachers, or others in authority can have a similar effect. So can being discouraged from following your passion or purpose.

When I moved to Scottsdale, Arizona the first time, I went out for a walk on the nearby trails, which border a golf course. I had my earbuds in my ears listening to music and thoroughly enjoying the sun and activity, when all of a sudden, WOMP! A ball driven from the golf course across the stream hit me right in the solar plexus. Thankfully my only injury was significant bruising - but I got the message: it's time to step into your power!

THE CHAKRA 3 BUSINESS TYPE

Chakra Business Type 3, Empowerment, is a business that helps people step into their personal power, which may involve overcoming fear, small thinking and shame. It may also help people shift from attempting to control outside circumstances to expanding their vibration to fully serve.

Examples include presentation or speaking coaches or trainers, life coaches, confidence coaches, bodyworkers, and breathwork coaches.

CHAKRA 3 CLEARING & ACTIVATION

See marciabench.com/cca-book-resources for the clearing and activation process for Chakra 3.

CHAKRA 3 CREATION LAW: THE LAW OF ALIGNMENT

We have talked about the importance of making sure your chakras are cleared so your energy can be aligned, both in creating your offerings and in marketing and selling your programs to clients. The Creation Law of Alignment goes even further to say that your intentions, your thoughts, words, and actions must be aligned in order for your desire to manifest.

Think of it as similar to building a house: if the foundation is not aligned with the frame, and the frame with the walls, it will not last.

So pay attention to how you talk about what you say you want. If you find yourself disparaging it or talking about how you don't think/believe it will happen, then watch out! You are neutralizing your intention with every word. If you say you intend to manifest greater abundance, then demonstrate your pride in your appearance, your home, your car and your office, as though you already had that abundance in your bank account. That "acting as if" will bring your desired result to you more quickly.

BUSINESS TASKS ASSOCIATED WITH CHAKRA 3

So what business tasks correlate with the solar plexus chakra? They include:

- How to Create Your Conscious Signature System

HOW TO CREATE YOUR CONSCIOUS SIGNATURE SYSTEM

Many Conscious Experts with whom I have worked insist that every client's needs are different and at what they do with each client varies. However, inevitably, when we closely analyze it, there are several core elements or steps or strategies that each client must complete in order to achieve the desired transformation or result.

One of my clients, Teresa, was juggling the time-consuming work of executive recruiting with executive coaching, and realized she too needed to find a way to systematize at least some of her services, to have the lifestyle and time freedom she desired.

Another client, Karen, a nutritionist, was booking clients for individual sessions with her, charging by the hour, but not engaging them into additional work with her - based on her findings in the initial hour - that would improve their nutrition and health. As a result, she was working seven days a week and being grossly underpaid for her services.

There are definite drawbacks to only offering hourly sessions and charging by the hour instead of using a Conscious Signature System, regardless of your specialty.

- **Your revenue will be uneven, and it will feel like a roller coaster.** You will only be paid when you are actively providing services, and there is no continuity month-to-month or even week-to-week that keeps your clients coming back and keeps your bank account filled.

- **You'll be working constantly to fill your practice.** Working in this "hours for dollars" model is designed to lead to overwhelm and frustration. First, you need to work hard to find people to meet with to become clients and then, once you have clients, you have no time to market to fill the pipeline with additional prospects. This is not sustainable long-term.

- **You will get lower quality clients.** Thirdly, the clients you do get will be much less committed than those who are willing to work with you for three months, six months or more. They're also looking for a quick fix, rather than the lasting transformation you know is possible using your services.

In order to overcome these challenges and lay the foundation for a much more sustainable business model, we recommend that you create a Conscious Signature System.

So what do we mean by a Conscious Signature System?

"A Conscious Signature System is a predictable, replicable model for delivering your services – with a unique name that brands the system – to help the client or other user of your system reach a desired result and/or solve an important problem."

Your Conscious Signature System will consist of a series of benchmarks – i.e. common steps or strategies – that you use with each client. Ideally, it will mirror your own journey of transformation.

For example, my own 18-year journey to find fulfillment at work, by realizing my life purpose went through a number of stages. I began feeling restless, I needed to know the answer to the question, "Why am I here? What is my purpose?"

I realized I didn't know the answer, so I continued down my path by asking the adults in my life how I could discover my purpose. I read every book I could find on the subject, went to dozens of classes and retreats, and still came up empty.

I got very discouraged. But finally, when I started my first consulting business and began working with my first mentor, a combination of some of the questions that she asked me, and the work I had already done, finally brought me clarity. And it was not an accident that it happened as I became self-employed.

I would diagram that journey as in Fig. 13:

FIG. 13 - MY TRANSFORMATIONAL JOURNEY

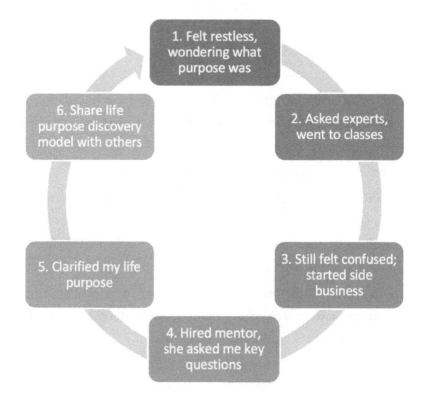

This transformational journey, early in my professional life, has become the foundation for literally everything I've done – from my 26 books, to my live events, online courses, globally recognized career coach certification and more.

BENEFITS OF A CONSCIOUS SIGNATURE SYSTEM

Some of the benefits of having a Conscious Signature System are obvious from this example:

- **No need to keep reinventing the wheel** – you go into each client engagement with clarity. You apply the proven steps that you have lived yourself to their unique situation, and they too are transformed.

- **You become known for it (legacy)** – as you will see below, one of the requirements of a Conscious Signature System is that it has a unique name. That name is something you become known for and helps develop your reputation within your field.

- **You can scale it to multiple income streams** – you can use those same five to eight steps to create a free sample of your services, an eight-week course, a weekend retreat or a year-long mastermind - or anything in between. The difference between the various offerings is the level of access to you.

- **Mixes passive and active revenue** – you are able to serve more of the people interested in your message. Those who can't afford your personal coaching services or your mastermind can still receive your entry-level products or programs. And this gives you passive revenue, along with contract payments from personal coaching or mastermind group clients.

- **Easier to enroll clients/more tangible** – selling a personal service - whether it is coaching, nutrition, personal training, or healing – it is intangible to the prospective client, until the services begin. When you can say that you have a proven system called XYZ that leads to ABC results and is delivered over a certain number of weeks or months, it is much easier to enroll them. It sounds more tangible and real.

- **Higher quality clients/more committed** – as you can see, when a client commits to multiple sessions, a group program or course, or a mastermind, they are committing to a result to a result, not just a certain number of minutes or hours with you. It is more fun to work with highly committed clients, and you will get better results.

- **Smooths out revenues** – finally, having a Conscious Signature System where your clients are committed to work with you for a number of months allows you to to devote the bulk of your energy to delivering an exceptional client experience, instead of constantly working to fill the pipeline. That's not to say there's no marketing involved at this point, but usually there is a launch period to fill the program followed by the delivery. In some cases, as you will see later, it is possible to have rolling enrollment throughout the year. Some clients will pay you up front and in full, while many will want to pay you month-to-month on an installment plan. It is much easier to forecast your revenue and make plans in your business when you have such advance commitments from your clients.

HOW TO CREATE YOURS

To begin creating your own Conscious Signature System, think about the journey that has led you to start the business you have now – or that you want to start. You should have articulated this in the last chapter.

Ask yourself these questions:

- What was your starting point?
- What steps did you go through in making the discovery that finally solved the problem or answered the question you started with?
- What did you try that didn't work?
- What was your breakthrough moment?

- What finally worked for you?
- What were the results that you realized at the end?

Now, diagram them in a cycle, as I did above. Do your steps describe a process? You may find that you have eight, 10, 12 or more steps initially, that you believe are essential. You'll want to combine the steps until you reduce it to no more than eight. More than that makes it sound too difficult for people, and it's also harder to scale it.

A CONSCIOUS SIGNATURE SYSTEM IS NOT...

People often think that their Conscious Signature System is a list of their services, e.g. coaching, seminars, books, workbooks, and videos. But these are not steps in a transformational journey – they are channels through which you deliver your services.

A Conscious Signature System is also not a list of the features of your product or service, e.g. six weeks, 10 sessions, online, in person, etc. And finally, a Conscious Signature System is not a description of your target market/Tribe, e.g. coaching for women in transition over 40.

Test yours and be sure that it is in fact a transformational journey, and you aren't running afoul of any of these traps.

WHAT ALL CONSCIOUS SIGNATURE SYSTEMS HAVE IN COMMON

Here's another way to think about it. There is an archetype known globally called the Hero's Journey. Carl Jung explored it in his work as a leading psychologist, and Joseph Campbell popularized it in the 1970's.

True Conscious Signature Systems follow the Hero's Journey steps. So does any great novel, movie, or other success story. There is a starting point where the leading character is struggling and has the opportunity to choose whether or not they will change. This is called the Call to Adventure (the word "Adventure" really meaning Transformation in our context). At the Threshold, our leading character says "yes" to the journey, having no idea of what lies ahead, but knowing they want the end result. A mentor then enters to help them (this may be YOU when it comes to your clients – it can also be a class, a book or a spiritual guide). They then go through Challenges and Temptations (the things they try that don't work, the people who derail them along the way, and their disappointments).

Finally, our leading character reaches the Abyss, where they give up. They may not believe change is possible, having run up against the wall so many times.

In this process, they surrender and die to their old self. Only then can the Rebirth occur and their new self emerge, transformed. This stage is the Revelation – it is the strategy or shift that does work for that person to achieve their desired result. For some people, the journey stops there and they simply enjoy the bliss of their transformation. For those of us called to service as I am, and as I suspect you are, we move into the stage called the Return. In this stage, we come down off our veritable mountain top and share our transformation with others, guiding them through it as well. That is the essence of our business and our Work.

This process is diagrammed in Fig. 14:

FIG. 14 - THE HERO'S JOURNEY

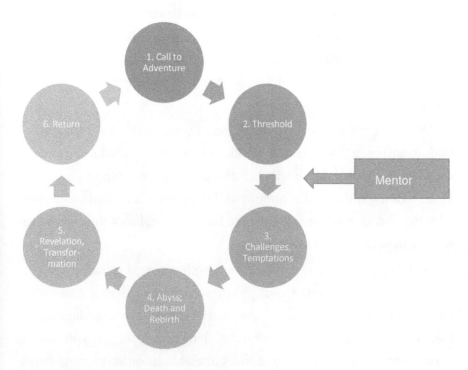

NOW, GIVE IT A NAME!

Your final step in creating your Conscious Signature System is to name it. You may decide to call your website by your domain name for the system, or you may simply want to own the domain and name your website something else. Many Conscious Experts use their own name for their website, to build visibility around their personal identity and/or expect to possibly shift focus and offer additional programs over the course of their career.

Be sure that the name of your system is results-oriented and not process-oriented. For example, relationshipcoachingwithkathy.com is process oriented; prosperduringdivorce.com is results-oriented. It should be a phrase that both combines the key attributes of your work and communicates something desirable to the prospective client.

Be sure not to type your proposed domain name into Google and if nothing comes up, assume that it is available. You must go to www.whois.com or a similar domain provider, enter the URL/domain name, and see if it is available for purchase. Millions of domains are held by individuals and parked for future use or sale, and you want to avoid using one of them.

Don't worry if your first combination of words is taken – keep playing with it until you find one that works. When I first started doing this, it took up to a couple dozen tries before I got a domain that was available. By cultivating my intuition and my ability to establish a soul connection with my clients, today it is usually the first or second idea that we end up using and which is also available.

Finally, once you find an available, result-oriented domain that you like, test it with a group of your prospective clients – does it mean what you want it to? Be sure to avoid any inadvertent hidden meanings before you commit to the domain long-term. However, I suggest you reserve it right away once you find one that's available in order to avoid being snatched up by a domain reseller.

COMMON BARRIERS TO CONSCIOUS SIGNATURE SYSTEM

Feeling stuck? You're not alone. I have noticed several common barriers that prevent my clients from being able to create their Conscious Signature System, including:

- **Taking your experiences for granted** – you have lived your own story, so it is easy to assume that others have had a similar experience. While many may suffer with the same problem, they haven't found your solution – they might not have found any solution at all. You could be their magic bullet. So trust that your experiences have value.

- **Feeling like it has to be "one of a kind" (though it will be)** – it is easy to become overwhelmed if you look at other people who have published books, done coaching, or are otherwise playing in the same sandbox you are. However, as long as you are not plagiarizing the work of someone else, and are modeling your transformation after your authentic experience, no one can argue with its validity. It will be unique simply because it is you and not someone else that is sharing it. As a business coach, I am one of more than 40,000 business coaches in practice today. However, the vast majority of them focus primarily on strategy, and not on the energy and transformational aspect of business. But for those that do, some clients are drawn to me versus another practitioner with similar background, simply because we are a better energetic fit. Trust that you will have the same kinds of results.

- **Wanting it to be "perfect"** – if you're anything like me, you don't want to share anything until you feel it is perfect. At least I used to be that way. And then, I adopted the strategy I call ready–fire–aim. Especially with our online world today, something that might seem perfect now will need to be changed next week or next month or next year to stay relevant. It is no longer sound business practice to spend months or years having something perfectly designed, edited and tested before we go to market. By that time, the market has already bought a similar service from someone else that was willing to go to market without it being perfect. Outline your steps and list of benefits to the customer or client, and then start sharing them. You'll be surprised how quickly you can attract clients through sharing your authentic experience and giving them hope. Have you ever bought a diet book just by hearing a friend's story of how it helped them lose ten pounds in a month or a similar result? That's the same principle.

- **Fear of sharing personal experiences** – finally, some people are uncomfortable sharing their personal experiences with their audiences – whether those are blog readers, attendees at a talk, or viewers of a Facebook live. I'm not going to ask you to do that yet, but just to hold open the door that with the right preparation, your most powerful work with your audiences, both online and off-line, will come from sharing the depth of your pain - as well as the highest reaches of your triumphs. Right now, simply identify those experiences and identify the key steps that you took to finally overcome your pain or solve your problem. There's much time ahead to prepare for making that public, to the extent that you are ready to do so then.

IS YOUR CONSCIOUS SIGNATURE SYSTEM READY?

If you are ending this chapter having articulated the specific steps of your own transformational journey that you can now share with others, you should be feeling excited. I am excited for you. This is one of the most pivotal steps you can take in attracting ideal clients that will be buying services from you – they'll actually be buying your story and the hope that your story provides a pathway for them.

Here are a few of the signs that your Conscious Signature System is ready:

- You're excited!
- People ask you, "Oh really, how do you do that?"
- You get consistent positive results.
- People start to seek you out – online and offline, as well as by referral.
- You can see how to build your brand into multiple products, services and variations of it.
- Your revenues smooth out and are growing.

Now that you have your Conscious Signature System, let's explore how to turn it into multiple ways you can serve your clients and prosper in your business.

CHAPTER 6

SECRET # 4: YOUR CONSCIOUS PACKAGING & PRICING

When Dr. Lynne first came to me, she was offering three-day weekend certification trainings in how to do healing. However, when she delivered her individual healing services, she would book clients for a single one-hour session - and they rarely renewed beyond that. She knew she needed to be able to grow and scale through packaging her healing services. And after making good money for years as a special education teacher, principal, and professor, she was frustrated because although she knew she had a lot to offer, she found herself constantly looking for clients.

I helped her create packages with her healing services, including a minimum required commitment of three sessions. She began speaking at metaphysical expos and hosting her own local gatherings. Using an offer sheet that followed the Conscious Client Attraction system, she has been able to make more money in the first six months of this year than she did in all of last year. And with her third book coming out in the fall, I know much more is ahead for her in the future. Packaging made all the difference for Lynne.

WHAT YOU'LL LEARN IN THIS CHAPTER
- Chakra 4 and Its Impact
- The Chakra 4 Business Type

- The Creation Law of Love
- How to Package Your Services to Meet Your Client Where He/She Is
- How to Confidently Charge Premium Prices

THE 4ᵀᴴ CHAKRA: HEART

WHAT THE HEART CHAKRA FOCUSES ON

The heart chakra is located at the center of your chest. Its focus, as you might expect, is on giving and receiving love, both to yourself and to others. The extent to which you show up authentically, unapologetically, and without holding back in any of your relationships – whether personal or business – has everything to do with how healthy this chakra is.

When the heart chakra is healthy, relationships thrive. Someone with a freely rotating heart chakra is a person to whom you are irresistibly drawn and want to get to know better. You can tell they accept and love themselves and that they will bring their full self to any relationship they have.

In the beginning of our businesses, our level of passion is usually quite high for what we want to create. There is the energy of newness, of creation manifesting – and we shower our fledgling business with love.

However, over time, that passion can ebb or get lost in the layers of systems and structures that are required for many businesses to grow. The minute your heart goes out of your business or a particular offering, your clients will pick it up right away at an unconscious energy level. Our passive growth, if we are to be business owners for the long haul, is to continue to reignite our passion without confusing our audience.

HOW TO KNOW IF THE 4TH CHAKRA IS BLOCKED

When the heart chakra is blocked, you will notice that you feel resentment or anger toward yourself or others. You may have trouble starting or keeping relationships – especially close ones.

Heart chakra blocks can also cause low self-esteem, depression, and feelings of rejection (when in fact you need to give that love to yourself). You may observe that you stay "in your head" when talking with and being around others.

You may lack the needed discipline to stay out of dysfunctional or co-dependent relationships that only partially meet your needs. Or you may surrender to addictive relationships with people or substances, in a vain attempt to get your needs met.

In short, there is something lacking in most, if not all of your relationships - if they are not grounded in self-love.

In a business sense, you may feel isolated, separated, and as if you cannot connect as deeply as you want to with your prospective Tribe members. You will feel like you're just "going through the motions" because the focus is on the surface/intellectual level in your marketing and sales, instead of on the heart/soul level.

WOUNDS THAT CAN BLOCK CHAKRA 4

So what kinds of wounds cause the heart chakra to get out of alignment?

These wounds can start quite early in life. Perhaps, like me, you were the oldest child in the family and an overachiever, acknowledged for what you can do, but discouraged from authentically sharing any feelings of inadequacy. Or, you might be the middle or youngest child in the family and feel like you are living in everyone else's shadow, and there's no way for you to stand out.

Any time a significant person leaves us unexpectedly and without notice, a heart chakra blockage can result. This could take the form of a parent leaving the family at a young age, death of a loved one, divorce, or an unexpected break up of a marriage or primary relationship. These experiences definitely leave scars that need to be addressed. They need to be healed, not only for our personal well-being – but also for the health of our business relationships, since they reflect our personal emotional health. The last thing our clients need, if we are their coach or healer, is someone who is codependent or depending on the client for self-validation.

Another type of wound at the heart chakra level is experiencing conditional love, where a parent or partner will only love you if you act a certain way. Consider this quote from Dr. Wayne Dyer:

"You may feel infinitely worthy of attracting to yourself material and spiritual prosperity, but **if you are not living the way of unconditional love you are interfering with your ability to manifest in your life.** In order to be divinely aligned with this universal infinite energy, you must become unconditional love."

—*Wayne Dyer, Manifest Your Destiny*

Often, when the giving or receiving of love is blocked, what will clear it is forgiving the one whom you believe did you wrong. Remember, forgiving is not saying they are right or forgetting the incident – it is a healing process designed to help YOU and clear your energy. You may write a letter that you do not mail, or visualize saying you are sorry to them (especially if they are no longer alive).

THE CHAKRA 4 BUSINESS TYPE

Chakra Business Type 4, Lover, is a business that helps people embrace love – self-love, love for one's intimate partner, or universal love for all of humanity. It may also help people express love in the form of charging what they are worth, finding their mate, or attracting their ideal tribe in a compassionate way.

Examples include relationship coaches, dating services, life coaches, financial coaches and financial planners, law of attraction coaches, and others.

CHAKRA 4 CLEARING & ACTIVATION

See marciabench.com/cca-book-resources for the clearing and activation process for Chakra 4.

CHAKRA 4 CREATION LAW: THE LAW OF LOVE

The Law of Love reminds us that the most powerful force in the world is love. Love can dissolve hatred, resentment, fear, and other difficult emotions.

Bringing love to the relationships we have with our clients, instead of simply seeing them as a number on a spreadsheet or transaction to be completed, brings a much higher perspective to our connection. The giving and receiving of love are one activity, as discussed above. Our job is to keep the flow going, even if we disagree with another person, believe they have wronged us, or feel irritated by their personality. Deep inside, we are all one, as we will explore in chapter 10. Being willing to bring love to every situation helps us to access that connection and see how we are much more alike than we are different.

Holding onto any resentment or lack of forgiveness keeps this law from working in our lives, and it also blocks our personal heart chakra. Cultivate the practice of love and ask yourself how you can love instead of judge. That simple act alone will begin to transform the world.

BUSINESS TASKS ASSOCIATED WITH CHAKRA 4

So what business tasks correlate with the heart chakra? They include:

- How to Package Your Services to Meet Your Client Where He/She Is
- How to Confidently Charge Premium Prices

Let's discuss each in turn.

HOW TO PACKAGE YOUR SERVICES TO MEET YOUR CLIENT WHERE HE/SHE IS

PACKAGING YOUR CONSCIOUS SIGNATURE SYSTEM

Once you have designed your Conscious Signature System, your next step is to create packages of services from which your clients can choose in working with you. You will want at least two levels so you can meet clients where they are now, as well as up-level them as they grow and their needs evolve.

MATCHING YOUR SERVICE PACKAGES TO CLIENT NEED & STAGE OF ENGAGEMENT

Before we consider how to structure and price your service packages, it is important to understand the psychology of the client's journey in deciding to work with you.

Most clients go through three levels of engagement - and some rise to a fourth level – in their relationship with you, as illustrated in Fig. 15. It parallels the experience of dating. Just like you would not normally ask someone to marry you on the first date, it is usually inappropriate to ask someone to spend thousands of dollars when they first connect with you.

People enter our Tribe and community first as Suspects. No, that doesn't mean they have a criminal background! It means they are new to you and your work and aren't sure yet whether or not what you have to offer is right for them. It's like seeing someone across the room that looks attractive, until you get a closer look. Then, you're not sure whether or not you want to strike up a conversation.

Once they pass through this Suspect phase – and we will talk in a moment about how you help them do that – then they become a Prospect. They have said "yes, I want to know more." The Prospect is now looking for a match. They are asking themselves (usually unconsciously), can this person relate to my situation? Do they have a solution to it? Is it the right solution for me?

Assuming the answer is yes, they will move through this stage and become a Client/Customer. This means they have spent anywhere from one to $1 to as much as $1000, depending on your overall system, which we will discuss below. You will notice that in Fig. 15, the 4 Stages of Client Engagement, Client/Customer is the longest one. This is because there are usually several levels of an investment and commitment through which they can move as they work with you. In a relationship, this might be represented by a coffee date, followed by a dinner date, followed by a weekend out of town.

Clients who absolutely love your work then elevate to the level of Evangelist. This is the equivalent of becoming engaged and married in personal relationships. Evangelists stay with you for the long-term, attend all of your webinars and live events, and bring their friends. They promote you to others. Because you have helped them change their lives, they want to share the transformation that you offer with everyone they know. This is usually anywhere from 5 to 10% of your total Community or Tribe, and they are a highly valued asset, as you can imagine.

FIG. 15 - 4 STAGES OF CLIENT ENGAGEMENT

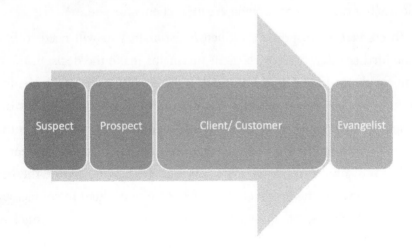

MATCHING OFFER TO CLIENT ENGAGEMENT STAGE

What you offer must be appropriate to the stage of the relationship you currently have with that person.

To convert a Suspect to a Prospect, you will offer them something tantalizing that is free so they can sample your work. This is sometimes referred to as the pink spoon concept, pioneered by Baskin-Robbins ice cream. Their research found that of all of the people who walked into their store, 85% of those who asked for a taste of ice cream on one of their little pink spoons would buy some kind of ice cream, even if it wasn't the one they sampled.

In the world of coaching and other expert services, the pink spoon takes the form of a special report, a short video series, a tip sheet, or some other piece of content introducing them to your approach. In order to get this content, they must opt in. It is critical that you create your title, the colors, fonts, and other branding to relate to them and their archetypes, as we have previously discussed. That way they have an instant positive reaction when they see the offer for your free content. Online, you have only 10 seconds or less to keep their attention long enough for them to provide their name and email address. If you are presenting a breakout session at a conference, you will be one among several other sessions offered during that same time frame. You will want to be sure that your title reaches those attendees who are ideal clients for you.

To convert a Prospect to a Client/Customer, you will need to have some further interaction with them that helps make the decision that is right for them. In the world of coaching and similar services, a webinar leading into an entry-level offer is often used for this purpose. Inviting prospects to participate in a one-on-one discovery session is another strategy, whether from a webinar or from another piece of content or a talk. And some cases, buying a book such as this one can be the next step that converts the Prospect to Client and invites them to contact you for further services. Many of our Certified Career Coach students have enrolled in the certification as a result of first buying my career coaching textbook.

The ascension from Client to Evangelist is somewhat less defined. It usually results from several positive experiences with you, coupled with outstanding personal results from what you offer. It is important that we acknowledge the Evangelists we have and nurture and encourage them to continue their relationship with us.

Fig. 16 illustrates suggested offerings at each stage of client engagement and recommended pricing as well. We will look in more detail at what fees you should be charging later in this chapter.

FIG. 16 - MATCHING OFFER TO CLIENT ENGAGEMENT STAGE

Stage	Suspect	Prospect	Client/ Customer	Evangelist
Goal	Lead Generation	Entry Level	Core Programs	Implementation
Example	Special Report, Video, Tip Sheet	Book, Online program, Silver package	Webinar series, online course, live event, Gold package	Platinum package, mastermind, VIP day, train-the-trainer, certification
Price	0	$1 - $297	$298-$2499	$2500+

HOW MANY LEVELS SHOULD YOU HAVE?

The diagram above refers to Silver, Gold and Platinum service packages. Whether you are starting out with business model one, individual coaching, (see chapter 3), or offering one of the more advanced group coaching models 2 through 5, you will still need two or three levels of services based on your Conscious Signature System.

Some marketing research shows that when you offer three levels, 66% of people will choose the middle/Gold level, some will want only your Platinum offer, and others will want to sample you at entry/Silver level.

However, as the marketplace becomes more crowded and people are faced with thousands of marketing messages every day, we do them a service, as providers, to make it simpler for them to choose. The trend now is to offer only two levels, usually a Gold style and a Platinum style package. If a Silver level is offered, it is strictly online, downloadable content, rather than individual or group time with you.

Fig. 17 illustrates a common structure for each level. The benefits of each lower level is included in the level above it – so Gold includes Silver, and Platinum includes both Gold and Silver benefits, as well as what is listed for Platinum. The levels do not have to be named after metals - they can be various kinds of jewels or other names related to your brand.

Remember, you will want to bring your own heart energy, love, and awareness of your market needs to the table as you design your packages. Also, we recommend that you provide bonuses at each of the services levels that add value and help the client more easily implement what you're teaching them. As an example, one of our common bonuses is my Million Dollar Resource List of pre-screened vendors, software, and other systems that our clients and students can use in their own businesses.

FIG. 17 - SAMPLE COACHING PACKAGE STRUCTURE

	Silver	Gold – includes all Silver benefits plus:	Platinum - includes all Gold benefits plus:
	Entry level online program	3 months of support	3 additional months of support
		Biweekly group coaching sessions	
			Six 1:1 sessions
			VIP day (4 hours)
Bonus	E-book	E-book	E-book
Bonus	Tip sheet	Tip sheet	Tip sheet
Bonus		2 tickets to live event	2 tickets to live event
Bonus			2 live 2-day retreats
Bonus		Private Facebook group	Private Facebook group
Value			
Price (1/4 to 1/3 of stated value)			

To design your own packages, use our Conscious Packaging Worksheet at marciabench.com/cca-book-resources.

HOW TO CONFIDENTLY CHARGE PREMIUM PRICES

You'll notice that we left the actual prices blank on Fig. 17 above. The reason for that is that prices – or investment levels as we prefer to call them – vary widely depending on:

(1) Your industry

(2) Your market

(3) Your experience

(4) What the market will bear

(5) The way you value your transformation

(6) Your level of confidence in charging premium prices

There is both an art and a science to setting fees for professional services. When you are using business model number one, individual services, you are trading time for dollars. And you'll tend to get more questions about your fees per hour, and more pushback on your overall pricing, with this model [remove comma here] than with any other.

I remember the relief I felt years ago when I discovered there was a formula for fee-setting, regardless of which business model you're using. It originates from the consulting industry, so we do need to make some adjustments to use it in coaching or other services. Once you get to the group coaching and mastermind models (4 and 5), you probably won't use the daily labor rate calculation as often. But it is good to know what you need to be earning on a daily basis on average to meet your revenue goals.

WHAT HOLDS MANY ENTREPRENEURS BACK

Whether you choose to use our Fee Setting Formula or not, it is critical to your business growth and success that you charge fees appropriate to the transformation you offer. There are number of factors that go into this, which we will discuss below. If you charge the equivalent of $100 or less per hour as a professional service provider, you will always struggle. Yes, there is a lot that needs to be done in your business, some of which you need to do, and much of what you need to delegate. I hired my first virtual assistant within the first 90 days of launching my online coach training company, and it got me into the habit of asking for administrative help. I have a background as an administrative assistant, and I continue to learn more about the various software systems that we use as my business has evolved. But if I tried to do all of those details and serve my clients and market and write this book and promote our programs, the business and I would suffer. My attention would be diverted from the most important tasks in the business, such as providing mentoring services and overall strategy and direction.

THE VALUE OF YOUR TIME

What is your time worth? For most people, even their most recent salary is not an accurate representation of the value of their services.

Consider the value of:

- Your education and certifications.
- The life lessons you have learned.
- On-the-job training.
- And most importantly, the value of your transformation to your client.

I remember sitting in a seminar not too long ago where a young man in his early 20s stood up and shared how he recently charged $20,000 for an hour's worth of work. Most of the audience members were entrepreneurs in their 30s, 40s, 50s or beyond. For their benefit, the seminar leader asked the young man how he could feel comfortable charging such a high fee. The man said, "I showed the client how making the one shift I was going to show him would generate at least $200,000 in the following 3 to 6 months. I was simply asking him to pay 10% of those results." That logic made perfect sense, and he paid the fee on the spot.

I would invite you to think about the value of your service beyond the focus of the services themselves – and definitely beyond the wage or salary structure of your prior industry. For example, if you are a career coach, of course your services help clients with their job search and work satisfaction. But it will also impact their finances including where they live, what kind of house they buy, what college their children go to, what cars they drive, and much more. But also consider how it will transform their family relationships by improving their satisfaction. It may also restore their faith in a Higher Power. it could even have an impact on their fitness and health. Wow!

Therefore, in considering the value of your services, make four lists: what kinds of positive benefits will your client have in the areas of:

(1) Faith

(2) Finances and work

(3) Family and other relationships

(4) Fitness

When you consider all of these aspects that can be changed by finding a more satisfying and well-paying job, healing the trauma of sexual abuse, successfully navigating divorce, or mastering the art of social media in one's business, it could be staggering. And it literally may be worth multiple six figures to your client if you can help them see what is possible when they finally find the solution that you have to provide. Your fee can be a set package amount or a percentage of the total value, as the young seminar attendee did.

FEE SETTING FORMULA

Let's start by determining what kind of annual income it will actually take your business to meet your needs. Too many entrepreneurs think only in terms of paying their personal bills and forget that there is business overhead, profit margin, taxes, and retirement savings to figure in as well.

See marciabench.com/cca-book-resources for our detailed Fee Setting Formula. For the purposes of our journey right now, let's take the big picture overview.

First, you need to determine what you want your net income to be from the business in the next year. That is, what amount will you take home from the business to use in your personal finances for your rent or mortgage, groceries, utilities, and other personal bills? If you want it to be the same as your most recent salary that's fine, but add a factor of at least 20% for the benefits and overhead the company was covering for you.

Second, determine your business overhead. These expenses will total more than you think, even if you're running a home-based business online. Examples would be your virtual assistant and any other staff; the various software systems that it takes to host webinars, do online calendaring, and track your finances; office supplies and equipment; any social media advertising or other promotion that costs money; your Internet connection, etc.

Total those two factors for the initial subtotal, as illustrated in Fig. 18.

FIG. 18 - FEE SETTING FORMULA - STEP 1

Now, choose the amount of profit you would like to make. Anywhere between 10 and 20% is acceptable. Add that to the first two items for your Annual Revenue Goal. (See Fig. 19.)

FIG. 19 - FEE SETTING FORMULA - STEP 2

CALCULATING DAILY LABOR RATE

You're almost there! Now, divide your Annual Income Goal by one of these:

- **Number of working days** – decide how many days during the year that you actually want to work. Out of 365 days there are 104 weekend days. Let's assume you don't want to work weekends in your freedom-based business. Taking those out leaves us with 261 days. Let's also assume you'd like to have some vacation, let's give you three weeks, which is another 21 days out of the equation bringing it down to 240 working days. If your Annual Revenue Goal were $100,000, your Daily Labor Rate would be $416.67, working 246 days a year. Meaning that every day you work, you need to be sure you bring in at least $416.67 to meet your goal.

We can get a little fancier and deduct marketing and administrative days as well and then bring them back into the formula as part of your overhead, but I think this calculation gives you a way of having a specific daily goal to work towards. Of course, it probably won't end up being $400 per day – it might be $1,200 one day and $100 the next– but if your averages on a weekly basis are around $2,000, working five days per week, you'll get there.

- **Number of private or group clients at x price** – I think it is good to know your daily goals regardless of how you structure your programs. But the other thing I like to do with my clients is play with the Annual Revenue Goal so it becomes more achievable. If it sounds easier to get to, you are more likely to manifest it. For example, to earn $10,000 per month, you could attract:
  - 1 client at $10,000 = $10,000
  - 2 clients at $5,000 = $10,000
  - 4 clients at $2,500 = $10,000
  - 10 clients at $1,000 = $10,000
  - 20 clients at $500 = $10,000
  - 500 "clients" at $20 = $10,000 (I put "clients" in quotes because at this price point they're buying a book or low end product so they are actually product purchasers).

Which would you rather have? At which price point are you most comfortable now? How many prospective clients do you want to be talking with during the month, knowing you will enroll anywhere from two to four of every five, depending on your skill level? Note that the investment level you charge depends much more on whether *you* believe you can actually get it than it does on the client. Much of it has to do with mindset. If you believe that your 90-day program is worth $10,000, you can sell it for that. Even people you wouldn't have thought could afford it will eagerly invest in it if they believe it will get them the answers they need. On the other hand, if you're not there mindset wise and your confidence wouldn't support that investment level, then start at $2,500 or even $1,000, and work up from there.

- **Number of seminar attendees or members or product purchasers at y price** – what if you sell books, journals, memberships at $27 a month or tickets to live events (which could range from $25 for a half day to $5000 or more for a 3-day exclusive intensive)? How do you figure those into the equation? If that is your primary business focus, then you need to do your numbers based on the number of sales at those prices that will get you where you want to be. If the volume is low, you will need to find a way of enhancing the price point for your products or low-end services or implement one of the group coaching models instead. What I like to do is use my coaching and training programs to meet my monthly goal, and any book sales, event ticket sales, or ala carte offerings are simply additional frosting on the cake.

The bottom line is, plan to meet your Annual Revenue Goal with whatever your core service is, and let other things fill in around it.

OTHER FACTORS THAT AFFECT PRICING

Other factors to consider as you set your prices, whether individual or group programs are:

1 – What the "competition" (what we call Related Providers) is charging – While there are definitely some providers that can charge $10,000 when everyone else is charging $1,000, they always have a reasoned strategy for charging those fees. You need to be aware of the marketplace and the typical value exchange so you can position yourself accordingly. It is almost never a good idea to position yourself as the lowest price provider (Wal-Mart being the huge exception to this in retail) because someone else will always come in lower than you.

2 – Your geographic market and location – One of the delightful benefits of being able to work online is that we are not bound by geographic area. Shortly after I started my coach training company, my husband I moved to the small resort town of Lake Havasu City, Arizona. I built the company from there for five years and had no students or clients in that city, or in the entire state of Arizona. It was all built online, and students enrolled from around the world - but not necessarily locally. So if you have been thinking that because you live in X location, you cannot be successful or charge a certain fee level, it is time to rethink that in view of the global business that is possible through the Internet. That being said, I do have some clients that prefer to brand themselves for their local area, e.g. chicagocareercoach.com or arkansasbusinesscoaching.com. (These are both fictitious names given as examples.)

In the consultant space, fees can vary from location to location. The cost of living in a place like San Francisco is markedly higher than somewhere like Wichita, Kansas. But once you start doing business online, geographic locations do not necessarily affect the fees you charge. However, you may charge different fees to different markets. Be sure that if you do so, you have a policy for why you do so the Federal Trade Commission does not have an issue with your pricing structure. For example, when we work with workforce development centers that are serving disadvantaged workers through a partially government-funded entity, we charge lower fees for them and their staff members to complete our certification than we would to the public. We also offer volume discounts if multiple people want to coach or train with us in one block or series. These are a couple of ideas you might apply in your own market.

3 – Your uniqueness, additional qualifications, and experience – Finally, you may charge lower or higher fees based on how unique your services are in the market. Be careful if you're offering something that seems to have never been done before (unless it is a scientific or medical breakthrough or similar idea) – there may be no one doing it because there is no money in it. However, there may be no one doing it because they haven't thought of it yet! How much education have you obtained in order to get the expertise you have? How many years of experience do you have that adds value to your clients? All of these can add to the level of fees that you're able to charge.

PRICING YOUR CLASSES

Pricing an eight-week webinar series or similar class structure requires that you determine the break-even point, after out-of-pocket costs and your time invested in facilitating the course. During the class, you will be providing them with live training sessions, workbooks, videos, and a private Facebook group, as well as bonuses.

For every hour you spend teaching, you will probably spend two hours preparing, at least when you are initially writing the content. You will likely have a virtual assistant or client concierge to support you during the launch of the class – which usually lasts three to four weeks – and to answer questions and provide support on the technical side for your students once they are enrolled. You may also have expenses for software for videoconferencing, graphic design of any materials, hosting of any membership portal, etc.

The rule of thumb for someone with less than 10 years' experience as a trainer or coach – at least in the online space – is to charge full tuition price of $997 and early bird discounted enrollment at half price or $497. If you are more advanced than that and have been doing this a while, depending on your audience and the kind of offer you are providing, you may be able to charge as much as $1,997 as tuition for a 5- to 8-week course. Many people will include tickets to their live seminars, workshops or events as a bonus to their online course. Run the numbers to see how many people you would need to enroll to cover your cost, times three or more, so you make a great profit. Then, design your marketing accordingly to reach the number of leads and prospects that will yield that result.

PRICING YOUR GROUP/MASTERMIND PROGRAMS

When you offer a group coaching program or a mastermind group, you need to value many more elements besides just your time and professional services. In these kinds of programs, members receive comprehensive support for a stated period of time, whether that is three months, six months, or 12 months. In the case of a mastermind group, they will receive monthly live training sessions, monthly Q&A sessions, workbooks, videos, a private Facebook group and bonuses, as well as access to the leader through Instant Messenger, the option of 1:1 coaching, and quarterly live intensive retreats with the group.

Setting the investment level for this type of group must be customized to your goals and the way you choose to deliver the group. If your quarterly intensives are at five-star luxury resorts, with extensive printed materials and a full-time client concierge to support your clients throughout the year, your fees will be much higher than if you choose to have virtual quarterly retreats and downloadable materials exclusively.

Typical mastermind group fees start at $20,000 per person per year and go up to $100,000 dollars per year or more. Consider your offering, your Tribe, and the lifestyle you desire and be sure to get some coaching or mentoring support when you're ready to offer this kind of the group so you don't make an expensive mistake.

RAISING YOUR FEES

There are right and wrong times to raise your fees.

Each year you offer the same group program or mastermind, it is natural to raise the investment level by 10 to 20% the next time you offer it. If however, you're using that as your entry-level program that people go through in order to access your higher-level VIP and mastermind programs, then you may want to keep it the same year-by-year.

The best times to raise your fees are:

(1) When you are too busy to take on more clients!

(2) At the beginning of the new calendar or fiscal year.

Whether you cite inflation, a new policy, a new version of your program, or whatever the justification is, it is more easily received at the beginning of a new year.

When you raise your fees, be sure to grandfather in existing clients by giving them advance notice and, if they will renew before the date your fees are to go up, they can have one additional year at the old fee level.

Now you have your service packages created and priced. It's time to start enrolling clients!

PART 4

CONNECTING WITH YOUR TRIBE

CHAPTER 7

SECRET # 5: YOUR CONSCIOUS COMMUNICATION & OUTREACH

"Just 13 years ago, I was happily married, living in a beautiful home in the San Francisco Bay Area, working as a Technical Recruiter at one of the premiere staffing firms in the nation, and seemingly on top of the world. Every area of my life appeared to be working well. I was married (and although my ex-husband and I were on opposite schedules, we planned weekend getaways on his off weekends). I had wonderful friendships with women from the church and other groups. I even had my own group running from home called Praying Wives, where we prayed for family and friends. At work I handled the technical contractors who were on a major project for the company. And at church, I supervised a children's ministry.

"Then my husband ran off with the church secretary.

"I went from anger to shock, to anger and back again.

"On top of that, my church relieved me of my position in the children's ministry and I found myself questioning my core beliefs about life, God, and everything. I also lost my job – and it felt like life as I knew it was coming to an end.

"Looking back, I wish I'd sought out support from friends, mentors and others – but I didn't.

"Instead, I found myself making poor choices for a period of time, including moving to a new state without researching it, burning through a nice savings cushion, travelling the world, incurring debt, and entering relationships with men who were not right for me.

"I wanted to turn my experience into something good by creating a container of support for women experiencing midlife transitions. I made several attempts to build a business. I created the Life Makeover Series, inviting subject matter experts to come in and speak on various topics pertinent to women experiencing common midlife transitions. Each time I put on an event, multiple cancellations and delays would occur with speakers. I took it as a sign that I needed to develop my own system of support and not leave my clients vulnerable to others.

"Marcia invited me to join Conscious Client Attraction Blueprint class at just the right time. I went from having no idea where to begin, and no content or delivery system, to designing Life Realignment for Women, launching in 2018, with my first retreat in the month of October. I have shared my retreat casually with women around the Bay area who are interested and excited. I have already reached my goal number of participants and am considering inviting more. I also recently started a Meetup group that already has 50 members and is attracting more women daily. This movement is on fire!

"I have learned in weeks what may have taken years to learn, under the guidance of Marcia Bench. I am able to see how I can multiply this business into many income streams. I now know that it is far better to attract clients than to chase them."

— *Germaine Robinson*

WHAT YOU'LL LEARN IN THIS CHAPTER

- Chakra 5 and Its Impact
- The Chakra 5 Business Type
- The Creation Law of Attraction

- How to Attract Your First 5 Clients
- How to Gather Your Tribe Online and Build Your List
- How to Build Your Online Presence
- How to Market Offline Through Speaking and Networking

CHAKRA 5: THROAT

WHAT THE THROAT CHAKRA FOCUSES ON

The fifth chakra is located at your throat, just where your Adam's apple is. As you might expect, it relates to how you communicate. Specifically:

- Are you speaking your truth?
- Are you being clear, or are you masking your truth in an effort to be liked?
- Are you willing to say what is really going on in a relationship or with a client - what Gay and Kathlyn Hendricks call the Microscopic Truth? (That is, are you focusing on what you're actually experiencing in the moment and not assigning meaning to it as you do so?)

When your throat chakra is clear, you can boldly speak your truth in your personal and business relationships, without fear of reprisal. If others disagree with you, it does not cause you to pull back inside of yourself and retreat. Rather, you understand there are many perspectives on the issue being discussed. You can allow both to coexist, and trust that you are attracting the people that are divinely matched to you.

There is great freedom in being able to confidently speak your truth. Your heart chakra below the throat and your third eye/intuition chakra above the throat coalesce here. When they are aligned, you can speak with both love and higher wisdom.

In the business context, your throat chakra is represented by all marketing and public relations activities. Any means you use to connect with like-minded people that are prospective clients for your services, buyers of your products or attendees at your events, require a clear throat chakra for you to most easily attract them.

HOW TO KNOW IF YOUR 5TH CHAKRA IS BLOCKED

When your throat chakra is blocked, you feel shy, withdrawn, anxious, and perhaps arrogant. These feelings simply mask an internal feeling of inadequacy and provide a sort of distraction.

You will find yourself holding back what you really want to say, as well as the truth about how you're feeling if you are afraid that it will be rejected. Tremendous internal insecurity can result, as you fear what others think and refuse to say what's true for you.

In your business, you will know inside of yourself that you have a great service and a viable offering, but you will have trouble telling others about it for fear of rejection. You may hold back in putting together your website or doing a launch because you don't want people to criticize you. In a more established business, you might notice that your marketing is now feeling stale and inauthentic and in need of a facelift.

WOUNDS THAT CAN BLOCK CHAKRA 5

So what kinds of wounds cause the throat chakra to get out of alignment?

At an energy level, many women entrepreneurs who are now called to speak their truth in providing their services feel a vague sense of fear when it comes time to do that. Some intuitives will say that we have incarnated through lifetimes in which we were burned at the stake (or worse) for speaking up. The wounds from our past life experiences are activated whenever we get on stage, start a webinar, or get on a sales call with client.

Whether or not you believe in reincarnation, it is easy to understand how experiences of being ridiculed, being put down, being punished for speaking up when you weren't supposed to, or having your beliefs or ideas mocked or made fun of, could cause long-standing throat chakra blocks.

These blocks must be cleared for you to courageously speak your truth in business.

I had an experience in the third grade - which one of my classmates always feels the need to point out at our class reunions - which, coupled with my natural shyness, has definitely led to fear in certain speaking situations. We were learning how to diagram sentences - to identify the nouns, verbs, adjectives, adverbs and the like. I thought it was a lot of fun and picked it up quickly. Many of the students were struggling with it. So one day the teacher asked me to come up in front of the class and teach sentence diagramming to the group in her absence. If I could do it over again, I would have said no, but even at that age I knew I was destined to be in front of audiences - so I said yes and taught the lesson. Needless to say, that didn't make me very popular with my classmates.

Another wound occurred later in life, during college. I reached the point when I could no longer tolerate my childhood religion. Every cell in my body screamed that I needed to get out, and I did – and had no idea what I would believe from that point on.

Slowly but surely, I was introduced to a more expansive and inclusive way of thinking by my college roommate and others. But simply making the decision to leave my traditional religion cost me my best friends and alienated me from my parents for a full year. Time has healed that wound, but still causes me to default to teaching business structure and strategy, instead of the spiritual and energy concepts I love, when push comes to shove.

THE CHAKRA 5 BUSINESS TYPE

Chakra Business Type 5, Teacher, is a business that helps people speak their truth – whether that is in their family relationships, in their job, or in their business. It may also help people overcome shyness or introversion, anxiety or physical throat problems that have an energetic base.

Examples include presentation or speech coaches, bodywork practitioners, healers who work with relaxing breathwork and inner wounds, and more.

CHAKRA 5 CLEARING & ACTIVATION

See marciabench.com/cca-book-resources for Chakra 5 Clearing & Activation meditation.

CHAKRA 5 CREATION LAW: THE LAW OF ATTRACTION

Simply stated, the Law of Attraction is the principle, "That which is like unto itself is drawn." The energy you put out comes back; what you focus on multiplies. This law is active in each of our lives, whether we realize it or not. So when you focus on getting into better physical shape, you notice diet plans, fitness regimens and people who are fit. When you start shopping for a new car, you pay more attention to every car on the road, especially the kind that you would like to buy.

Before we come to understand how it works, we may see ourselves as the victim of circumstances. But when seen through the lens of the Law of Attraction, we realize we have drawn certain people and situations to us for our learning and growth. If we want to change the kind of people and situations we attract, we simply need to change what we are focusing on day by day.

There are three steps in the Law of Attraction, according to *Ask and It Is Given* by Esther and Jerry Hicks:

1. **Ask** – State your desired outcome, whether it is a thing, a person, or a state of being.

2. **It is given** – as soon as we state our intention, it is already done in the invisible world. There's a Bible verse with a similar principle that says, "before they ask, I will answer." If we can stay out of the way long enough, step three will occur.

3. **Allowing** – our desire manifests in physical form.

Wayne Dyer puts it this way in *Manifest Your Destiny*, "The central notion of manifesting is the understanding that you have within yourself the ability to attract the objects of your desire…

"[H]umans never create anything. Our function is not to create, but to attract, combine and distribute what already exists. Creations are really new combinations of already existing materials."

The first time I read that passage, it truly comforted me. I realized I did not need to invent something out of nothing through my intention or through my desire. I simply needed to invite a rearrangement of what is already here. That makes it sound easier, doesn't it?

DESIRE AND EXPECTATION

Stating our desire and realizing it are often two different things. To become someone who regularly obtains the outcome of your desired intention, you must expect that your good is on its way. This expectation should carry forward so that, as much as possible, you're living as though it is already here.

Raymond Holliwell puts it this way in *Working with the Law:*

"The underlying law that regulates supply in the world of effects has two important phases; one is 'desire' and the other 'expectation.'…Desire without expectation is idle wishing or dreaming."

"[W]hen you constantly expect that which you persistently desire, your ability to attract becomes irresistible. Desire connects you with the thing desired and expectation draws it into your life. This is the Law."

Napoleon Hill makes similar statements in *Think and Grow Rich*. I bring these other experts into our conversation to show there is consensus about what works when it comes to the Law of Attraction. Rather than debate the merits of the validity of this Law, simply put it to the test. By asking, expecting, and receiving, even with something simple at first, you can see for yourself that it works. I have manifested everything from clients and money to cruises, houses, my soulmate, and even my dog using this Law.

In business today, where people are bombarded with over 5,000 marketing messages per *day*, it is critical that you "attract them to you," instead of "marketing at them." Give them content they can't refuse, share stories they relate to, and show them how you can help them get the results they crave.

WHAT CAN IMPEDE ATTRACTION?

There are three common impediments to attracting whatever you desire in your life or business. First, after you state your desired outcome, many people begin doubting, worrying, or fearing that it will not happen. Those three emotions essentially neutralize your intention. Worrying shifts your outcome to affirming what you do not want, instead of what you do want. This is the primary reason that most of us need to repeat our intentions daily and look at vision boards or similar pictures of our desired outcomes. It is not to persuade the Universe to provide them to us, but to program our focus to stay on our desire.

While you are focusing on that outcome, live as much as possible as though it has already happened. Feel the freedom of having all the money you desire to spend and all the clients you desire to serve. That doesn't mean running up a bunch of credit card debt claiming you are financially free. But it does mean not getting all upset over a $.50 discrepancy in a bill.

A second common barrier to attraction that I notice among my Conscious Expert clients is that they change their mind too often. There's a saying in the twelve-step movement, "Don't give up before the miracle." You may have heard it as, "It's darkest before the dawn."

In other words, if this month they put one offer out or use one marketing strategy and don't get the results they were hoping for, next month they completely change their offer and use a different marketing strategy. Fabienne Fredrickson calls this the "short order cook syndrome." It's like going into a diner, ordering a ham sandwich, and then five minutes later, calling the waiter back to change your order to a salad - and then wondering why your meal hasn't arrived.

Getting seen and connecting to your ideal Tribe members online takes time and persistence. And while I do not encourage you to keep using a strategy that is getting no results, do focus on what is working instead of changing course completely. Give each strategy and offer enough time to work.

A third barrier is getting derailed by others who are not entrepreneurs and do not understand the Creation Laws. Even though they mean well, your family members and friends will at times think you're crazy. When you share your dreams and ideas too soon with people who are not on the same wavelength with you, your doubts will be amplified by their feedback. Consciously surround yourself with like-minded people who are also using the Creation Laws to create results in their life. This is one of the reasons I have created my coaching groups and live events – to provide a forum for all of us together and support each other in moving forward.

BUSINESS TASKS ASSOCIATED WITH CHAKRA 5

So what business tasks correlate with the throat chakra?

They include:

- How to Attract Your First 5 Clients
- How to Gather Your Tribe Online and Building Your List
- How to Build Your Conscious Online Presence
- How to Market Offline Through Speaking and Networking

Let's discuss each in turn.

HOW TO ATTRACT YOUR FIRST 5 CLIENTS

Our work thus far has focused on helping you identifying what kind of company and brand you will create, who you will serve, how you will help them step-by-step, and how you will package and price your services. Now, it's time to introduce your amazing services to the world.

As we embark on the marketing part of our journey, I wholeheartedly agree with the definition of "conscious marketing" given by Carolyn Tate in *Conscious Marketing: How to Create an Awesome Business with a New Approach to Marketing:*

"Conscious marketing is all about building something so fundamentally good and compelling right into the heart of your business, products, and services that everyone wants to join your tribe and spread the word."

Eventually, you will have your own website, social media pages, launch strategy and more. But when I work with clients, I emphasize the fact that **you do not need a website or other sophisticated online presence in place, in order to get your first few clients.** In fact, insisting on having a perfect website at this stage, before you start reaching out to enroll clients, can be a delay tactic. It is a perfect way to protect someone from the fear of speaking the truth. Ask yourself if you might have already been caught in this trap.

One of my prior coaches, a very successful wealth coach, purposely left a very ugly looking website up for two full years, as he filled his live events and his coaching masterminds well into the seven figures. This was to prove the point that one's website is not the be all and end all that people think it is, any more than one's resume makes or breaks a job search.

I am a huge proponent of what I call the ready-fire-aim method. In other words, move forward with the information and guidance you have, don't get bogged down with all kinds of fancy systems in place before you take action. The world of online commerce and expert services simply moves too fast for that.

So if you don't need a website, how do you get started?

Begin by dedicating the next 30 days to filling your practice with at least five new clients. Whether you have a new practice or you've been at it for years, it takes focus and prioritization to literally breathe life into your business in the form of new clients. If you have volunteer commitments or optional activities that could be deferred for a month, then do so. Have someone else walk the dog, get the groceries, do the laundry and clean the house. Engage your family's support and the support of those around you whom you trust by telling them you are focused on launching or expanding your business, significantly over the next 30 days. Ask for their support.

You will be relying on two primary strategies to enroll these first five clients:

1. Networking - online and in person.

2. Discovery calls, aka strategy sessions.

Be sure you first have a very clear idea in your mind of who your ideal prospect/Tribe member is from our work in chapter 6, and that you have made a list of the associations, meetings, groups, media channels, podcasts, and other places to find them. Then, embark on this journey with enthusiasm and confidence – you are about to attract your first few clients and help others break through as you have!

Take the time to create a vision in your mind of those first five ideal clients. Affirm that you are now attracting them to you. You can enroll them on the spot. They are looking for you. Whenever you feel stuck along the way – either enrolling these first five clients or doing a sophisticated launch later on – come back to your vision and see yourself attracting irresistibly that next client or that next $5,000 or whatever it is that motivates you. The Universe will meet you where you are when you state that intention and take action to bring it into the physical reality.

1. NETWORKING

Networking is one of the easiest ways to initiate a relationship with your prospective clients. The key is to cultivate warm prospects by focusing on a commonality you have – whether that is a past working relationship, the sport your kids share, or the industry or interest around which the networking group or association was formed.

a. Connecting with Leads.

Start by preparing to reconnect with everyone you know now or have known in the past. The best Conscious Client Attraction is usually done with warm contacts, not cold contacts, although there are exceptions.

Open a fresh screen on your word processing program or a fresh spreadsheet or a fresh piece of paper, and list everyone you know, past and present. Do not do any screening in terms of whether you think they would be candidates for your services – each one of these people knows 50 to 500 others. So don't worry about qualifying them now. What's important is that you want to be able to chat with them, based on a current or prior relationship.

Now, setting that aside, go back to your list of the trade associations where your Tribe gathers, especially those that have local meetings. Calendar the meetings that are happening in the coming month and plan to attend. If there are Chambers of Commerce, Meetups, other industry groups or professional networking groups (those that don't require weekly or monthly dues) you can identify through a quick Google search or through searching meetup.com, make note of their meetings and planning to attend. You should be going to at least two of these meetings per week during this focused client attraction period.

Remember, when you do attend these events, don't just wander in and hope something good happens! Be very intentional. Choose the events you attend with care, and before you go in – I often do this on the drive to the meeting – state your intention for how many people you want to meet and obtain contact information from (and ideally an expression of interest in your services) by the end of the meeting.

b. Setting Appointments.

i. *Current and prior contacts.* Set aside time every day to reach out to the people you know and have known in the past, by phone. Phone is the best, text message or Facebook or LinkedIn instant messenger second best, and email last in terms of effectiveness. Your goal is to first genuinely connect from the heart chakra with them, find out how they are doing. It might be a quick text that says, "Got a minute to talk?" or "Let's catch up – you free now?" Then, after the connection is made, say something like this,

"I wanted to reach out to you because I didn't know if you realized I [have started] or [am expanding] my business into the area of _____. I am specifically looking to talk with people who are seeking resources in their finances [or whatever your specialty is]. And I wondered if anyone in your sphere fits that situation?"

I love this approach because it is not asking if that person wants coaching or if they know anyone that wants coaching, but instead, is asking them for a referral.

If they say yes, ask them if it is okay for you to use their name when you call the person. Ideally get their email address as well. If they say no, they can't think of anyone, then be sure you have their current email address and send them a summary of your services, without listing prices, through email for them to keep in mind for future situations.

ii. *New contacts met through networking* - when you meet someone at a networking event, you do not want to have an in-depth discussion of what you do and their needs at the meeting. Instead, set a time at the meeting to meet - both of you can check your online calendars on your phones while you are there. Otherwise, be sure you have their contact information and get back to them the next day. Never leave it in the hands of someone you meet to follow up with you! Once the connection is established, you want to be the one to deepen it.

2. DISCOVERY CALLS

When you are about to meet with a prospective client – whether over coffee or on a conference or phone line – be sure that before you meet with them, that you have a summary of your service packages ready to show them when the time is right. You would never begin the meeting with it on the table – rather, you would show it to them once you begin talking about a specific offer (step four of the Conscious Conversations to Clients Roadmap we discuss in the next chapter).

Then, simply move through the Conscious Conversations to Clients Roadmap in your conversation with them and you will find a certain number saying yes.

Fig. 20 illustrates how quickly this can turn into cash for you:

FIG. 20 - CLIENT ATTRACTION WITHOUT A WEB SITE

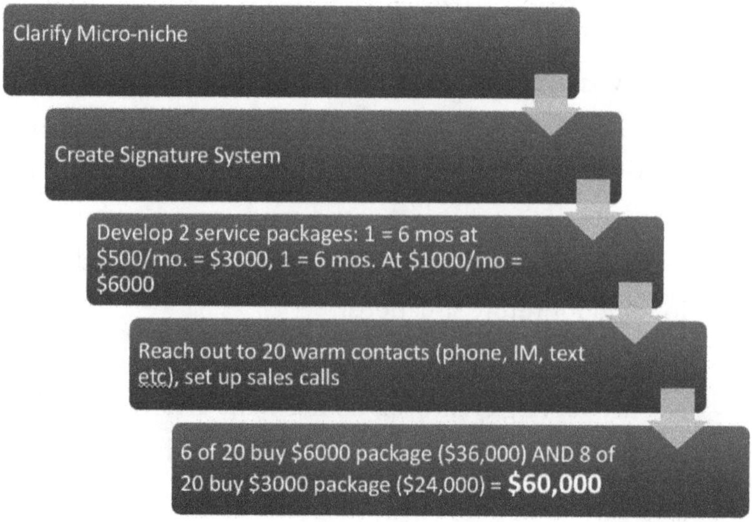

Clarify Micro-niche

Create Signature System

Develop 2 service packages: 1 = 6 mos at $500/mo. = $3000, 1 = 6 mos. At $1000/mo = $6000

Reach out to 20 warm contacts (phone, IM, text etc), set up sales calls

6 of 20 buy $6000 package ($36,000) AND 8 of 20 buy $3000 package ($24,000) = **$60,000**

And this is before you do a webinar, a live talk, or run any ads! Those strategies can multiply your results quickly once honed. How would it feel to earn an extra $60,000 from a few phone calls?

Even if the exact numbers are overly generous, what if you sold $20,000 using this method in the first 30 days? It just takes a willingness to reach out to people, connect with their need, and show them the pathway to a solution.

HOW TO GATHER YOUR TRIBE ONLINE AND BUILD YOUR LIST

Now that you have some momentum and hopefully a few clients already committed, the next step is to create a more structured process for attracting clients that ultimately you can put on autopilot to an extent.

It can be a bit daunting once you begin to become aware of all of the different strategies – and the software programs and apps that go with them – by which people obtain clients and leads. Therefore, in this chapter, we are going to reduce all of that confusion to a simple seven-step system that you can use, even as you continue reaching out by phone, text, and instant message to leads online.

The beauty of online marketing is that you can do it from anywhere and reach people anywhere. I grew my coach training company to span 50 countries around the world from a meager beginning in a small town in Arizona, where I had no students or clients in the entire state. I got into coaching when my husband retired and we wanted to travel. Therefore, I could no longer have a job that required reporting to an office. Online marketing and online program delivery provide such an amazing amount of freedom that we have been able to literally see the country and the world, while still running my business.

LAUNCH MODEL VERSUS ROLLING MODEL

There are two primary models for marketing your coaching services, which are Launch and Rolling.

The Launch Enrollment Model is used widely in the industry and popularized by Jeff Walker. It requires that you prepare several pieces of content - usually including several videos and free downloads - in advance of a webinar. Following the webinar, there is a brief period when your shopping cart is open and you accept clients or students into that program (which can be your private coaching, an event or a class). After that period of time, the program is closed for enrollment until the next launch. Usually, once you have refined your process and demonstrated success by doing a few launches yourself, you would then invite partners to promote your free content and webinar, and pay them a percentage of the sales come from their referrals. This is called affiliate marketing. We will not be addressing that in great depth here, but refer you to the book *Launch* by Jeff Walker if you're interested in implementing this model.

What I like about the launch model is that it does focus your marketing efforts in a specific period of time. However, it can be very exhausting, especially when you have a lot of partners and perhaps thousands of registrants to manage. You will most likely use the Launch Model to begin with, until you hone your content and are steadily converting prospects and clients, just because it gives you a real-time feedback about what works and what doesn't.

Then, there is the Rolling Enrollment Model. In this model, you automate your process so you are bringing in new leads and converting them into clients throughout the year 24/7, as illustrated in Fig. 21, Rolling Client Attraction Sequence. You begin by creating a central place to attract a group of like-minded prospects, such as a Facebook group. Using a combination of strategic posts and live videos to them, as well as sharing similar content by email with your primary mailing list, you begin to enroll clients. Then, you create Facebook ads and use other online portals, such as YouTube and Twitter, to draw people matching your Tribe criteria to you. Then, you send them to an automated webinar, running at specific intervals throughout the day, on demand, every day. You may be asking them to enroll directly into a class or to commit to a discovery call with you as a result of the webinar. That sequence, running 24/7, brings in a consistent flow of leads, and simply requires you to use our Conscious Conversations to Clients method to convert them to clients and scale your business.

Regardless of which model you're using, it is all about attracting and engaging your prospective clients by providing content to which they relate. Just as meaning has become the way we distinguish brands from each other, stories and content have become the way we choose professional services. This is not limited to experts like us – everyone from insurance companies to plumbers, carpet cleaners to roofers now initially engage their prospect with a free useful information packet, and then make the sale. This approach establishes trust and facilitates an easier sale.

FIG. 21 - ROLLING CLIENT ATTRACTION SEQUENCE

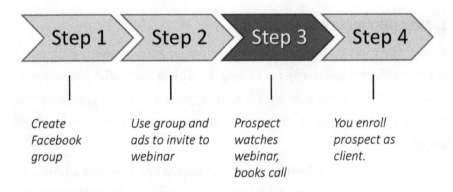

Step 1	Step 2	Step 3	Step 4
Create Facebook group	Use group and ads to invite to webinar	Prospect watches webinar, books call	You enroll prospect as client.

7 STEPS FOR ONLINE CONSCIOUS CLIENT ATTRACTION

Let's look at each of the elements of online Conscious Client Attraction, as diagrammed in Fig. 22, individually so you can start attracting clients online now.

FIG. 22 - 7 STEPS FOR ONLINE CONSCIOUS CLIENT ATTRACTION

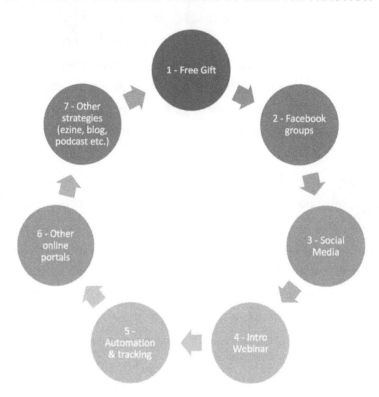

1. FREE GIFT AKA LEAD MAGNET

One of the tools you will use throughout all of your marketing strategies is a free gift, also known as a lead magnet. This is the initial content your prospect will see, whether they're joining your Facebook group, opting into your mailing list, or expressing interest in you following a speaking engagement you presented.

No doubt you have downloaded these yourself online – most commonly people use special reports, white papers, manifestos, free videos or free self-assessments as their free gift. The main factor that determines whether or not your prospect will say yes to your free gift is the title. It needs to promise a solution to an urgent and current problem.

The best titles include a number, some of the copywriting power words such as secrets, discover, revealed, etc., and close by handling a potential objection with the phrase "even if…" Examples:

- Painter: Report on "How to Choose the Right Paint Color for Your Room – Even if You've Never Painted Before"
- Chiropractor: "5 Key Questions to Ask Your Provider to Avoid Making Your Injuries Worse – Even if You're Afraid of Chiropractors"
- Divorce Coach: "3 Important Questions to Ask When Considering Divorce – Even if You're Afraid to See a Lawyer"
- Health Coach: "4 Secrets to Losing 10 Pounds Before Thanksgiving – Without Giving up Carbs – Even if You Have Tried and Failed at Dozens of Diets Before"

The primary goal of your lead magnet is to give your prospective client a sample or introduction to what you do by showing how you solve the specific problem your services are designed to solve – as we explored in chapter four. This is your "pink spoon." So consider one aspect of your services where your clients face the most painful and urgent challenge. This is what you want to focus on in your lead magnet.

Your special report only needs to be about 10 pages, double-spaced, with some graphics. It will start out by acknowledging the reader, sharing the promise of the report, telling your story, sharing the three or four main points of the report, and ending with a call to action. This is by far the easiest type of lead magnet for most new Conscious Experts to create. The added value is that the process of writing it is an excellent exercise in laser focusing on what your clients need most.

It will then be uploaded to your website and accessible through an opt-in page, once your prospect provides their name and email address. You will use an email management service, such as Aweber, Constant Contact, Get Response or one of the others listed in our resource list on the book resource page at marciabench.com/cca-book-resources to capture the contact information of your prospects.

You will not only make this gift available at your website, but provide a link to it any time you speak, on your Facebook business page, on your Facebook lives, in emails, and anywhere else you want to engage people.

2. FACEBOOK GROUPS

One of the best ways to get your tribe interacting with each other while you position yourself as a Conscious Expert is to form your own Facebook group. These groups, which are free to create and free to join, give you an additional community with which to share your message. The primary advantage of this over email is that you can interact and post many times throughout the day with people in your group, whereas if you sent that many emails it would upset them.

When you do your launch, or as part of your rolling enrollment system, you will post the free content you create to the group. You will also want to encourage people to join the group by putting the link to the group on any thank-you pages for opt-ins to free gifts or webinars, as well as at the bottom of your email signature, on handouts at workshops, and anywhere else your content appears.

You will want to be sure you establish rules for the group that prohibit members from promoting their own programs within your group. Your Facebook group's objectives are connection, sharing resources, and encouragement, but not self-promotion by its members. We recommend you require people to answer three prescreening questions before joining the group. This can be done in settings when you establish your group. This allows you to learn a little bit more about each member so you can start a dialogue.

Be sure that you also brand your Facebook group by creating a custom URL. The name of the group should be aspirational so that it speaks to the results your clients are seeking. For example, two of our public Facebook groups are Conscious Client Attraction and Career Coaches with Passion and Purpose.

3. SOCIAL MEDIA

Another way to introduce your services to people you know, as well as attract other like-minded people, is to use social media. Chances are, you already have a page or presence on one or more of the common social media platforms, such as Facebook, LinkedIn, Twitter, Instagram, or Pinterest. Eventually, you'll want a page for your business as well. But you can do a lot from your personal page to begin with.

Be creative and think of ways you could do an online grand opening of your coaching, nutrition, healing or other services – or the release of a new book or program.

- Create a Facebook event for your grand opening and invite people to it with intriguing short messages leading up to the event about what is coming.

- Do a series of daily or every other day posts or Facebook live videos, each with a theme of a common problem your Tribe faces. Then invite them to the grand opening.

- If you know other people who provide related or similar services to yours, then invite their Tribe to your grand opening, assuming it is noncompetitive to that person's offerings.

- Arrange for a well-known celebrity or provider within your space to either record an endorsement ahead of time that you can play on your grand opening or have them interview you during the grand opening.

The sky is the limit when it comes to intriguing and enticing promotions. Some of my colleagues are finding that spontaneous, off-the-cuff posts with an almost, "by the way" announcement that they're going to share a resource in a few hours is a powerful way to attract the right people.

Then hold your grand opening. If you do it on Facebook live, be sure to optimize that video or boost the post so as many people see it as possible.

BEST PRACTICES FOR FACEBOOK POSTS:

When posting on Facebook, follow these guidelines to get optimum engagement:

- Post regularly – many people post daily – to your wall, as well as to any groups that you run

- Always use images in your post. Posts without images are not widely viewed.

- Make your posts provocative and invite interaction.

- Mix up short versus long, inside setting versus outside for photos or videos – keep things interesting for you and for them!

- Invite feedback and comments.

- Tie your posts to current issues, when possible, or to common problems your Tribe faces

In addition to boosting a post or turning it into an ad, consider posting that same content on Youtube, Twitter, Linkedin or other sites where you can enlarge your audience.

4. INTRODUCTORY WEBINAR

Short of live speaking engagements, webinars are the single best way to connect with and build rapport with your ideal clients. This was at least 75% of our marketing approach when I built my first online business to its current reach spanning 50 countries. Not only do they get to experience your approach and content, they get to experience you. They feel your energy, see how you speak and come across, and can easily make a decision about whether you are the right expert for them. The connection happens faster than by simply reading your articles, blog posts or hearing you on podcasts.

If you have never done a webinar before, it may seem like a lot of work, and the technology may intimidate you. But I require each of my

Conscious Expert clients to master this marketing method, because there's nothing that works better.

There are seven components you will need to implement to host a successful webinar that converts clients.

a. **Opt-in and thank-you pages.** First, you need a compelling page that provides your prospects with the title of the webinar and the key takeaways. Most people use a program like Leadpages.net or clickfunnels.com for this. We recommend you use the same approach for the title for your webinar as you did on the title for your lead magnet. The most successful opt-in pages are short and to the point, with just four or five key bullets of what the attendee will gain by attending. The thank-you page simply confirms the registration, provides the link for attendance and should include an invitation to your Facebook group if you have one.

b. **Slide deck.** Second, you'll need to prepare a series of slides in PowerPoint or Keynote that guide the attendee through the journey of transformation you have experienced and how you can help them. We usually have up to 50 slides for a one-hour webinar, in order to have a complete picture that in turn motivates the attendee to respond positively to the call to action. After beginning with the promise of your webinar, you will reassure the attendee they are in the right place and take them through three or four key points, with illustrations or case studies, that preview your approach. Then, you will show them they have a choice to either keep things the way things they are or to accept your invitation to change. Outline what that looks like and how to do it, and the webinar then ends. If desired, this can be divided into three shorter webinars, using the popular micro–learning approach.

c. **Technology/portal.** The third component is the service that you use to host your webinar. There are many services available, but by far the most popular and user-friendly at least as of this writing is

Zoom.us. It allows videoconferencing internationally, screen sharing, user chat, and recording, all of which are critical features for training online today.

d. **Offer page.** Fourth, before the date of your webinar, you will need to prepare a web page on which the prospects who wish to buy from you can do so. It may be a full long-form sales page, or simply an enrollment form with highlights of what your offer includes, as explained on the webinar. All payment links must be active and working properly, so be sure to test those before you do your webinar.

e. **Email engagement and follow-up.** The fifth component is crafting emails to engage people to join your webinar and to follow up with those who attended. Too many experts express disappointment when they host a webinar, perhaps due to a low number of sign-ups or show ups, and then they say it didn't work. But the truth is, with people's schedules today and the number of marketing messages they are sifting through, you are leaving most of your money on the table if you stop there. You will need to be creative over two to three weeks prior to your webinar, taking different angles in your emails to engage with prospective attendees, as well as afterwards. At least 75% or more of your sales will happen after the webinar. Be sure to follow up for anywhere from three to seven days afterward with a prepared series of messages.

We'll talk in the next chapter about strategic use of discounts in your sales activity. But that advice also applies here – offering early bird registration discounts, insider preferred rates for current clients, or disappearing bonuses that go away after a certain date are all incentives to get people to sign up with you during the 72-hour period following the webinar.

f. **Social Media.** The sixth component of a successful webinar is making effective use of social media. Whenever you send out an email to your list, you will want to repurpose it into Facebook and Linke-dIn posts, posts to your Facebook group, Facebook lives, YouTube videos, tweaks, and even articles. Daily communication is not too much when you are launching. One of the advantages of being able to transition to the Rolling Enrollment Model is that you do not have to post as often, since you are engaging new prospects from paid traffic. If you do not want to be doing all of your posting in real-time, you can use a service like HootSuite.com to pre-write and pre-schedule your posts.

g. **Affiliate Partners.** Finally, you may want to consider using affiliate partners with specialties that are complementary, but not competitive to yours, to help spread the word about your services and expand your reach into new groups of prospects. Of course, they will expect to be compensated with a percentage of sales results. This is most commonly used when promoting a course, as opposed to a coaching program or a longer-term mastermind, due to the price point. In some cases, affiliates will run their own paid advertising to garner leads for the campaign. This is an advanced strategy, but one that can definitely multiply your results when you are ready.

5. AUTOMATION AND TRACKING

Once you have hosted multiple webinars and are reliably converting clients from them, it's time to automate. By now, you will know how to craft your invitations, web pages, webinar content, as well as your follow-up to get solid results.

a. **Facebook ads.** By beginning to run Facebook ads to send people to your webinar, you will have access to an amazing array of statistics and tracking through your Facebook Ads Manager. This will allow you to further refine the language and images you use so you are attracting only those people that are ideal for you. The topic of Facebook ads could be an entire book alone – and indeed many have written books on that strategy. But it is the most affordable form of online advertising available and is highly customizable as well.

b. **Automated webinars.** Perhaps you have signed up for a webinar through an email or something that came across your social media feed where it appeared to be live, but you weren't sure if the host was actually there in real time. Automating your webinar through a company such as stealthseminar.com allows you to deliver your content day in and day out without you having to physically be there. Stealth provides you with useful tracking data on people who have started watching your webinar and how long they stayed. And what's even better, they do all of the programming and set-up, so there's no technology for you to learn.

Once you have all of the aspects of these first five steps working seamlessly, you will be able to relax considerably in your marketing because you will start to see a consistent flow of leads that will in turn result in a consistent flow of sales.

6. OTHER ONLINE PORTALS.

Many online marketers had a rude awakening with the recent Facebook scandal regarding data that was shared inappropriately during the election of President Trump. It's never a good idea to put all of your marketing eggs in one basket. Marketers need to diversify, just like investors do. Even public companies like Facebook and some of the other social media companies are not a panacea. They can change their algorithms any time they wish - or even shut down - due to unforeseen circumstances. Therefore, you will want to diversify your approach to Conscious Client Attraction by using other portals. Creating your own YouTube channel, LinkedIn page and group, and exploring Google Ad words are some of these strategies that can expand your reach and diversify your audience.

7. OTHER STRATEGIES AS APPROPRIATE.

There are at least five other online marketing strategies that you may want to incorporate into your plans to attract new clients. They are briefly summarized below.

a. **Ezines.** Ezines, also known as electronic magazines or online newsletters, were a stable in online marketing until recent years. They have largely gone out of favor, was many marketers preferred to focus on more ad hoc and less scheduled strategies. However, we continue to publish an ezine every Monday and have for the almost 18 years we have been online. Not only does it give us a chance to update our online community with useful content and recent developments - it also provides a non-promotional way to alert in our community of upcoming free webinars, live events, and other events of note. We can feature one of our books or products, a case study or a testimonial each week which, along with the main article, builds further trust and credibility with our community. We then repurpose that article into a blog post, which is published weekly. If you wish to see our ezine and be informed of upcoming events in our community, simply provide your information at marciabench.com.

b. **Virtual summits.** My colleague Milana Leshinsky invented the telesummit in the early 2000's as a way for experts to surround themselves with other experts in their field, and thereby position themselves as a Conscious Expert. Some people use summits to share alternative perspectives around a common theme or issue. The strategy took off and was very popular for a number of years - until it started to be overdone – or as Milana would say, done incorrectly. She has recently updated the concept into the "virtual summit" with several different variations and levels of complexity. It can be a fantastic way to establish yourself as an expert and build connections with other experts in your specialty, even if you have been practicing a long time and are ready to freshen things up. Since this is a specialized strategy, I will refer you to Milana's work at milana.com for guidance. See book resource page at marciabench.com/cca-book-resources.

c. **Blogging.** Many new experts believe that once they get their website finished, it will stay that way. But in fact, the food for the insatiable search engines is new content. Posting new entries to your blog once or several times each week will help you attract the search engines and therefore, more leads to your website. Blogging does not need to be complicated – we recommend you simply sit down and make a list of 52 or more topics representing your clients' hot buttons, pain points, and areas about which they would love to get further information. Those can be the topics you write about in your blog, and then repurpose into other social media platforms and videos on a weekly basis.

d. **Podcasting.** Being a guest on others' podcasts - or hosting your own - can be a fabulous way to expose your work to new people. While it is only audio and not video in format, it is very convenient for people sitting in traffic, in the gym, or with time on their hands when they would like to be learning. Simply do a search for podcast directories and the keywords for your specialty to find the best ones to approach to be a featured guest. John Lee Dumas is one of the leading experts in podcasting – contact him at eofire.com.

e. **Public Relations/Media Exposure.** Press releases are an underutilized strategy that can get you visibility leading to prospects and clients – at no charge. During my 10-month tour, I had notified the newspaper in my home city of my trip and that I would be back in town toward the conclusion of it. They arranged a photographer and reporter to come to me and published an article about my tour on the front page of the Living section of the paper just as I returned. It can also be useful to heed current news events and celebrity antics that might be able to be positioned in relation to your services. For example, if you are an expert on flipping houses and the Kardashians just sold one of theirs, you might be able to get coverage by playing off of that current event. It doesn't have to be anything that fanciful, but it does need to be relevant for you to get coverage on local television, newspaper, or magazine. And you will definitely want to use press releases to announce the release of a new book, the launch of a new program, a speaking engagement, and the like. For free services that distribute your press release throughout a wide range of publications, see the book resources list at marciabench.com/cca-book-resources.

HOW TO BUILD YOUR CONSCIOUS ONLINE PRESENCE

At whatever point you feel comfortable as you implement the seven steps just discussed, you will want to give close attention to your online presence and ultimately create a website for your business. But remember, with the ready–fire–aim approach, you can finance your investment in the website, logo and other branding from already committed clients, rather than advancing those before you start to market yourself.

As you consider what colors, thoughts, images and the like to use on your website and other social media platforms, keep your Brand Personality and its archetypes in mind. If your prospective clients do not see consistency in everything you do online, as well as relate to the brand archetypes represented, they will feel a subconscious disconnect - which can in turn cause them to doubt your credibility.

BUILD A BRAND BOARD

One of the most useful exercises you can do is begin to study the colors, fonts, arrangement of copy on the page, and images with which you resonate on other web sites. Begin to keep samples of those on a brand board like that illustrated in figure 23. That way, when you do commission a logo or web design, a picture truly is worth a thousand words. Designers think visually, and they will appreciate the fact that you give them something to look at to express what it is that you want.

Two online sites that are organized well to house your brand board are canva.com and pinterest.com.

FIG. 23 - BRAND BOARD EXAMPLE

YOUR CONSCIOUS WEBSITE

Think carefully about the purpose of your website. When used strategically for Conscious Client Attraction, it is not simply a brochure about you and what you do, but rather the central hub of all of your marketing efforts. It should work like an engine to convert suspects into prospects, and prospects into clients. Therefore, choose carefully what you do and don't include in the content.

Will you include your prices or not? For most experts, the answer is no, because they want to have an opportunity to explore the prospect's goals and challenges and customize a recommendation to them on a phone call.

Will you write your About Us page in first person or third person? That is, is it as though someone is writing about you, or as though you are telling your own story? We recommend the latter because your goal is to draw the visitor in and begin to build a relationship with them. It's much harder to do that with a more formal, third person biography. Also, consider the photos that you use on your About Us page – they should be warm and welcoming, while at the same time being professional.

SECRETS TO A GREAT DESIGN

I highly recommend you use a professional designer, rather than one of the DIY programs that are available. When you choose someone to design your website for you. ask them if they have done websites for other Conscious Experts like you. If they typically work for corporations or companies that sell products, rather than authors, speakers, and coaches, their approach will not be as relevant for you.

For your domain name, most experts choose to use their own name as the website name. However, as mentioned above, we want you to buy the domain that represents the title of your Conscious Signature System to avoid having someone else put it into use later, after you've invested years of branding and marketing around it. You may also choose to use that signature system for your primary website's domain name. But because we find most Conscious Experts launch multiple programs over their career, branding your Conscious Signature System can limit you. If you use your own name as your domain, you can launch multiple programs without having to have a new website every time.

Your website design platform should be Word Press. It is both user-friendly and search engine friendly, and is universally used for websites being put online today. Once that choice is made, you will then need to choose a theme for the design. Consult with your web designer about this decision.

Each of the key pages outlined below will of course need some copy to be written. Your web designer will not usually prepare this copy. When I work with clients, I usually have them prepare a draft of the copy and then work with them to revise it so that it has the right Conscious Marketing spin. It is time well spent to do some Google searches, and perhaps use a tool like wordtracker.com, to find out what phrases are most commonly used to search for services like yours. That way, you can build those phrases and keywords into your copy and the headlines on your pages, to help the search engines find them more easily.

The best way to learn how to write copy for your web pages as to emulate – but not copy – what you see others doing. Model their structure, but don't copy their language word for word. Make a list of the top 10 experts in your Micro–niche, study their websites, and come away with great ideas for your own. Just remember that every word of every website on the Internet is copyrighted. Therefore, do not make the mistake thinking you can just change the name, publish the copy on your website and call it yours.

If you don't feel comfortable writing your own copy, we recommend you contract with a professional copywriter to help you, perhaps through upwork.com or by referral from a colleague. The reason I have shied away from using professional copywriters over the years and decided to learn this art of copyrighting myself is that they are very expensive. They often charge as much as $10,000 or $20,000 to write a single sales page to make sure it converts it well. You do not need to make that kind of investment initially, as your website will be an ongoing changing document that evolves with you.

KEY PAGES TO INCLUDE

The primary pages you will want to include in your website are:

- **Home:** A brief introduction to you and your work, what is in it for them, and perhaps a few testimonials or recent blog posts.

- **About Us:** Share your transformational journey on this page with pictures showing them how you are able to relate to their current problem and how you have solved it. Don't make this stuffy.

- **Work with Me:** Also called the Services Page, Work with Me is a little more personal and invites the visitor, based on a brief overview, to book a session with you to discuss their needs and your services.

- **Resources/Free Gift:** As discussed above, you will want to have a special report, free assessment or other free gift that you can offer to anyone visiting your website. It should not only be a pop-under that appears after a few seconds while they're browsing your site, but there should also be a special page for it.

- **Blog:** Since you will be repurposing each Facebook live or post or article of substance into a blog post, you will need a blog page as well.

- **Contact:** Be sure to have a contact page with your company address and email. If you have a company phone number and want to include it - that is optional. Most websites today do not include that information. You don't want to convey the idea that you can be reached whenever someone wants to reach you. Instead, demonstrate that you are busy serving your clients and they will need to schedule a time to talk with you. A live calendar link through meetme.so or acuityscheduling.com is a great alternative for setting up strategy session calls.

If you have any books or other products, they can be put on a Products or "Store" page. And later on, you will add sales pages about specific offerings, and possibly an Events page if you're doing workshops, seminars, or retreats.

Be sure to think about how you want a visitor to move through your website by storyboarding the key pages. Be sure that at the bottom of each page there is somewhere else for them to go. Never let them land on a dead-end.

There are many plug-ins today that will allow your Facebook feed to be updated in real-time on your website, your blog posts to be updated as you make them - both on the blog page and on your homepage, live calendar links, and more. Consult with your web designer for his or her ideas on how to make your website interactive so that it's interesting to the visitor and attracts more traffic.

HOW TO MARKET OFFLINE THROUGH SPEAKING AND NETWORKING

As you can see, online marketing can be an amazing platform for you to use to draw from the millions of users worldwide. But don't overlook the importance of getting face-to-face with prospects through speaking and networking. This in-person or "off-line" marketing can play well into building your online community.

SPEAKING

There are some 77,000 meetings every day in North America – and you can be sure that your prospects are attending some of them! When you speak at professional conferences, local meetings, Meetups or other gatherings, you are instantly positioned as an expert with credibility.

When I started Career Coach Institute, I was a relative unknown. The way we established credibility quickly is by identifying the three major career conferences that occur throughout the year, submitting proposals to present workshops there, and being present as both breakout session presenters and exhibitors. That, along with weekly webinars, catapulted our business rapidly into the mid six figures in just two years.

Speaking is literally one of the top five most lucrative professions - as well as the most impactful — because people are influenced significantly by the words they hear. And they are always looking for good news and inspiration amidst the challenges of their day-to-day life!

Speaking can be both an additional profit center for your business and an opportunity to build your expert reputation and develop referral business. But since most people fear public speaking more than death itself, it is important to overcome fear to be able to take advantage of this outlet. One of the ways to do so is simply learn more about it.

When my clients are preparing to do their first presentation, they often feel somewhat nervous, anticipating the thought of sharing what is most near and dear to them. But inevitably, if you focus on connecting with the audience and sharing your transformational story of hope for them, you will discover that people appreciate your candor, they resonate with your passionate cause, and they want to join you in it!

DEVELOPING YOUR SPEAKING SKILLS

If you are new to public speaking, it is definitely a skill you will want to cultivate if you want to be the champion of your movement. I learned speaking largely by doing it — carefully observing other good speakers, then selling everything and taking my ten-month, 65-city seminar tour around the U.S. with my first book. You can bet the 65th seminar was quite an improvement over the first one!

To learn speaking, consider joining a local Toastmasters group — which are located in every city - hiring a private speech coach, or simply becoming more active in your professional trade association. Attending and getting involved with the National Speakers Association chapter in your area is also a wonderful place to gain "nuts and bolts" tips not only becoming a successful speaker, but on marketing yourself as well.

You can use your new or well-honed speaking skills in multiple venues as you develop confidence and experience and overcome your fear of speaking (if any) through practice. The outlets include podcasts, webinars, guest keynotes, live workshops, and multi-day events, among others.

Regardless of whether you speak virtually or live, the structure of your talk will be very similar. Just keep in mind the need to "edutain," as discussed in chapter 1.

Hosting live workshops, and multi-day retreats and training events can truly showcase your expertise while engaging clients into your programs at a higher level of commitment and investment.

NETWORKING

Another way to build your community and attract followers is through networking – but you need to be selective and strategic to avoid wasting time, money, and valuable energy in fruitless contacts or uninteresting meetings.

Think in terms of where the people that fit the definition of your Tribe are gathering – and plan to be there to meet them! (e.g. a coach attending a meeting of other coaches is *not* doing strategic networking, but spending time with colleagues – unless coaches are his/her Tribe); strategic networking would be attending a meeting of his/her prospective clients.

And to turbo-charge your strategic networking, volunteer for boards and committees in the organizations your Tribe attends. Nothing says Conscious Expert better than being a leader in one's professional association!

Some other tips for strategic networking include:

1. **Attend gatherings of your tribe's trade association locally.** Seek out the three most influential people in the room...and connect with them at the meeting and afterward for coffee or lunch.

2. **Meet industry leaders or heads of your Tribe's trade associations** – they can introduce you to others, meeting the definition of your Tribe.

3. **Attend conferences and apply to present a workshop** (the document will be called an RFP – request for proposals – or request for workshop presentations, and usually comes out three to twelve months in advance). Plan your workshop to lead naturally into a call to action to sample your services.

4. **Attend groups or form your own group of networking colleagues,** who share leads with each other regularly. Consistency is key to success, so you would plan to meet weekly or biweekly and give incentives for providing leads to each other in that context.

5. **Try to learn more about the people in the group before you meet,** and if you haven't connected online before you meet, request to connect with them afterward. Also, join the LinkedIn Groups they belong to.

Fig. 24 illustrates the many possible online and offline marketing strategies you could use to reach your prospects. Choose two or three primary ones in each column to focus on to get more people on your mailing list and, ultimately, on the phone to discuss hiring you to help them.

FIG. 24 - ONLINE AND OFFLINE MARKETING CHANNELS

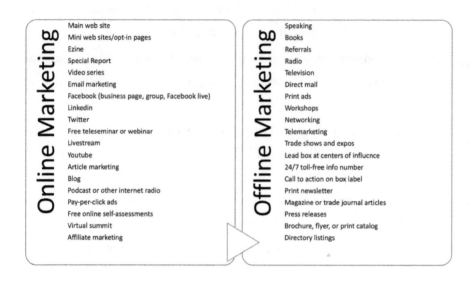

Great! Now you know how to market your services and communicate with your Tribe. But what happens when someone expresses interest? The next chapter guides you through the enrollment conversation.

CHAPTER 8

SECRET # 6: YOUR CONSCIOUS CONVERSATIONS TO CLIENTS/ CUSTOMERS

"About a year and a half ago I divorced my husband because he forged my name to more than $75,000 in credit card debt and a car, and cleaned me out financially. Near the same time, I lost twin babies, my two dads died and my cat of 18 years died. I was emotionally distraught and extremely depressed.

"I had been a recruiter for 28 years, but was burned out due to the income roller coaster. I moved to a new city and ended up getting a job to make ends meet. One time I had to put two quarters together to get cat food. The job wasn't what I wanted to do – I was used to working for myself and hated not having the freedom and flexibility I was accustomed to.

"I came across your career coach training and realized that was the one thing I still enjoyed: helping people with their careers. Therefore, I learned how to do career coaching, and then enrolled in your Conscious Client Attraction Blueprint, which showed me what was missing in my business. I lacked consistent lead generation and especially using manifesting and clearing the chakras to heal the past.

"I started my career coaching business, Career Coach Experts, and assembled a team of strategic partners. In just a couple of months, through regular lead generation and sales calls, I have attracted 24 private career coaching clients, some retainer clients and have doubled my revenue from my best month in the recruiting world. I wake up happy now, I'm able to travel, and I feel re-engaged in my life again."

— Melissa Beaudet

WHAT YOU'LL LEARN IN THIS CHAPTER

- Chakra 6 and Its Impact
- The Chakra 6 Business Type
- The Creation Law of Guidance
- Understanding the New Model of Sales for Conscious Experts
- Mastering the Conscious Conversations to Clients Roadmap
- Best Ways to Overcome "Objections" aka Questions
- Training Others to Expand Your Sales Team

CHAKRA 6 AND ITS IMPACT

WHAT THE THIRD EYE CHAKRA FOCUSES ON

The sixth chakra is located between your eyes, and is referred to as your "third eye."

It focuses on following your intuition, imagination, foresight and openness to guidance. It may include various spiritual gifts such as clairvoyance or clairaudience, or just plain "gut instincts" about a situation.

HOW TO KNOW IF YOUR 6TH CHAKRA IS BLOCKED

You know your third eye chakra is blocked if you find it difficult to set direction for your business – or your life. You may feel stuck, like something is holding you back – and unclear what to do next.

You may find yourself seeking safety in what's always worked and in the rules and regulations. You don't have time to innovate, meditate, and seek inner guidance about what is new that wants to emerge.

Your thinking may be solely linear versus holistic because you are not accessing your intuition along with your logical mind.

In a business sense, you may notice the results from your marketing and sales decline, as you become disengaged from your offerings.

WOUNDS THAT CAN BLOCK CHAKRA 6

So what kinds of wounds cause the third eye chakra to get out of alignment?

These wounds can include experiences such as being told your intuition is bad or not to be trusted, or following what you thought was intuition and having unexpected or undesirable results.

If you are a man, you may hold the belief that intuition is only the domain of women – but in the context of business this is not true. Women do have more physical connections between the two hemispheres of their brain, so they can access it more easily, but both men and women can train themselves to hear their intuition.

THE CHAKRA 6 BUSINESS TYPE

Chakra Business Type 6, Intuitive, is a business that helps people access their intuition and spiritual gifts (clairvoyance, clairaudience, healing gifts, etc.). It may also help people overcome repression of their intuition, creativity and imagination from childhood.

Examples include creativity coaches, spiritual facilitators who help activate spiritual gifts, angel readers, and visioning practitioners.

CHAKRA 6 CLEARING & ACTIVATION

See marciabench.com/cca-book-resources for Chakra 6 Clearing & Activation meditation.

CHAKRA 6 CREATION LAW: THE LAW OF GUIDANCE

Since the sixth chakra is all about accessing your third eye and intuition for guidance, it follows that the Creation Law related to it is the Law of Guidance. Guidance is always available to you, whether from God, your angels, or your spirit guide – but it is never forced upon you. You must ask for the guidance.

Don't wait until you're in a jam to do a "foxhole prayer" – instead, get in the habit of accessing your divine guidance daily. Once you can discern its voice, and how it uniquely speaks to you, you can receive insights about clients with whom you are working. You can help them navigate situations they face and make tough decisions. This will greatly enhance your ability to be of service.

HONORING AND FOLLOWING YOUR INTUITION

As Albert Einstein wisely pointed out,

"The intuitive mind is a sacred gift,

The rational mind is a faithful servant.

We have created a society that honors the servant

And has forgotten the gift."

The Western culture and way of doing business trample on the dimension of the intuition. Intuition can be messy, but it can also save a tremendous amount of time, money, and heartache. I define intuition as, "the capacity of knowing without the use of rational processes; keen insight." It refers to those times when you "just know." You don't know how you know, but you trust the insight.

Growing up, I was discouraged from following my intuition or even recognizing it was there. My mother was so intent on making sure I became a responsible person that logic became king. I don't fault her for that, since I know she was trying to avoid my living in poverty as she did. But I now know that logic is only half of the equation. Two of the biggest mistakes I've ever made in my life, with far-reaching consequences, came as a result of not following my intuition.

IS IT INTUITION OR YOUR AGENDA?

So how do you know whether it is really your intuition, or another voice from your logical mind?

Intuition is characterized by not being logical, but bringing you an insight that you wouldn't have thought of on your own. It usually won't ask you to completely change your life overnight, but rather take one small step that requires trust. You'll notice that it comes to you - you don't go seeking it.

On the other hand, your logical mind may come up with clever ideas that *seem* logical, but if they feel self–centered, would cause harm to someone else, or are just personal projections of your own situation onto another, they are likely not your intuition.

Start by practicing sensing your intuition on something simple, like checking in to see if you can tell who's calling you on the phone without looking at the caller ID. Or before heading out on an errand, close your eyes, get quiet, and see if there is anything you need to know. Sometimes I have had a sense to take surface streets, instead of the freeway, and find out later that I've avoided sitting in a long traffic delay due to an accident.

Then, during your sessions with clients, check in beforehand, as well as throughout the session, to see what your intuition is telling you that could help them.

BUSINESS TASKS ASSOCIATED WITH CHAKRA 6

So what business tasks correlate with the third eye chakra? They include:

- Understanding the New Model of Sales for Conscious Experts
- Mastering the Conscious Conversations to Clients Roadmap
- Best Ways to Overcome "Objections" aka Questions

- Training Others to Expand Your Sales Team

Let's discuss each in turn.

THE NEW MODEL OF SALES FOR CONSCIOUS EXPERTS

When we begin to talk about the idea of sales, many Conscious Experts cringe. "I got into this business to transform lives, not to be a salesperson!", they exclaim. And I understand. As an introvert myself, mastering the sales conversation has not come naturally. But whether we like it or not, every single one of us – expert or not – is in the business of sales. When you try to convince your teenager to make his/her bed, you are doing sales. When you try to persuade your spouse to go on vacation where you want to go, you are doing sales. And when you talk with someone interested in your type of services, the conversation inviting them to make a commitment to work with you is doing sales.

Because of the stigma around the idea of sales for many Conscious Experts, several years ago I began using different terminology for the process. Because it is simply a conversation with a specific structure to it, I now call it Conscious Conversations to Clients. We will explore the model in depth in a moment.

But first, we need to be sure that you are ready to have these conversations. In addition to understanding what questions to ask and how to lead the conversation, you also need to address three important subconscious aspects of the process:

1. **Your connection with your offer.** Now that I have been an online business expert for nearly 20 years, I have seen several of my brands go through the birth, maturity and death process. If you are a new business owner, you are birthing a new brand right now – and are 100% connected to your offer. But after you have been in business for a while, you may feel as though the services that you've been offering are getting a bit stale for you. Even though you don't realize

it, your prospective clients pick up on that. If you are becoming disconnected from or bored with your offering, they will be less likely to buy it. They won't know why - they'll just know they don't feel as enthusiastic as they would like to about it. So continue to check in with yourself and be sure you are still excited about what you're offering to your prospects. When your enthusiasm begins to wane, get into meditation and consult your guidance about what wants to emerge. As soon as you get reconnected to your offer, your sales will immediately increase.

2. **The B.S. Detector.** Yes, that means what you think it does. Because people are so bombarded today with marketing messages, they have developed a keen radar to be able to determine quickly whether someone is motivated by getting the sale or by true service. Enter your sales calls with the attitude of "How can I serve this person, whether or not they buy from me?" Your prospect's defenses will go down and your sales will go up. If you are feeling financially strapped or desperate for income, it is critical that you leave what one of my mentors calls your "money karma drama" outside the door during your sales calls.

3. **Yes's and No's.** No matter how talented you are in the client enrollment process, not everyone will say yes. For some, it will simply be a timing issue. Two years ago I had a sales conversation with a mentor that I really wanted to hire, but it just didn't feel right. The next week my mother had the first of her four strokes, and I ended up in a three-month, full-time commitment to her care. If I had said yes despite my hesitation, it would not have been good for either one of us. I did hire that mentor six months later and had a great experience. When the prospect says no to your offer, it is easy to feel like they're saying no to you and rejecting you. To protect your energy from these no's when they happen, focus on selling your system, not yourself. Know your conversion ratios. If on average it takes you four conversations to successfully get one client

commitment, then don't get discouraged after call number three. Even the Conscious Conversations to Clients system is a numbers game to an extent.

THE OLD SELLING MODEL

My father was an auto parts salesperson, and when my mother remarried after his death, my stepfather owned car dealerships. Needless to say, between the two of them and my own experiences in buying automobiles and other items, I've had my share of exposure to the old-fashioned, manipulative sales model. Not to disparage either of my dads, but they didn't have access to the new way of selling that is now required.

Studies show that women now make or influence 85% of the buying decisions in North America. As that percentage has grown, women have forced the sales process to become more respectful and humane.

In the era when my dad and stepdad were selling (up to about 15 years ago), the old sales process was characterized by:

- **Cold calling** – It was strictly a numbers game - the theory was that the more people you called, the more leads you would get. This is simply not true any more, due to the barriers of voicemail and caller ID – yet many companies still rely on this strategy.

- **Competitive, scarcity based** – The belief was that if you get your sales, I won't get mine, and vice versa. Therefore, it was quite cutthroat, and each person was protective of their leads, territory and strategies.

- **Aggressive** – Salespeople in the old model could get quite pushy, thinking that the more pressure they put on a prospect, the more likely they were to buy. Today, that simply alienates buyers.

- **"Bait and switch," deceive client** – It was quite common to have a "loss leader" offer at a ridiculously low price to get the prospect in the door, where they quickly discovered that that item had been sold out (supposedly). But then, they were encouraged to buy something else at a higher price. These deceptive practices are now illegal, but were commonplace in the old model of sales.

- **Overcome "objections"** – The prospect's objections – i.e. reasons they said they wouldn't or couldn't buy – were something to be overcome with a variety of canned strategies that today would seem comical.

- **"Close" the deal** – The transaction ended with the sales person closing the deal, which meant they had won the competition. Getting to the close went by names such as take-away close, assumptive close, urgency close and the like. The underlying assumption was that if you fooled the prospect enough, you could get them to buy, even if they didn't want to do so. Needless to say, if what you are selling is a transformational service, this is the exact opposite of what you want to do.

THE NEW SELLING AKA ENROLLMENT MODEL

Thankfully, there is an alternative. We're not really trying to sell *to* anyone, we are simply giving them the opportunity to enroll *in* one of our programs and commit *to* their own growth and development. This dynamic requires a much more respectful approach.

This new sales/enrollment approach is characterized by:

- **Warm contacts through content, referral** – Instead of calling anybody and everybody, hoping someone will say yes to a sales call, we thoughtfully create meaningful content and cultivate relationships with referral partners. Those channels generate warm leads, which are then given the opportunity to view our webinar or get on a call with us, if they believe it would be of value.

- **Cooperative, abundance based** – Replacing the old competitive dynamic is one of cooperation with an abundance mentality. Partnering with like-minded experts - and co-creating products or programs together - is increasingly common. We know from quantum physics that ideas, resources and matter itself is continually expanding, *ad infinitum.* Both you and I will attract the perfect clients for us. My perfect clients would not find you to be their ideal provider, and vice versa. There is no competition for your life purpose, as we have said before. Therefore, overly protecting one's territory is no longer the focus in the new model.

- **Authentic, respectful** – The new enrollment approach replaces aggression with authenticity, honoring the prospect as an equal. We talk with them in a respectful way, trusting that they know what is in their best interest. We know they may encounter some fear prior to making their decision to change. We don't put high pressure on the prospect.

- **Lead with genuine value, invite to go deeper** – We don't insult the prospect with a bait and switch approach, but instead offer them our valuable content through our marketing, each piece of which invites them to take the next step. This allows an organic growth of the relationship between us as the Conscious Expert, and them as the prospective client, which feels better to everyone involved.

- **Answer their questions** – We know that whenever a prospective client is about to commit to working with us to change their life, they will have questions. That is what objections are. So we don't try to overcome them, we help them answer and move through them. Then we point the prospect back to the goals they stated earlier in our conversation if they start to doubt themselves. This will become more obvious as we go through the script below.

- **Enroll/invite client to commit to him/herself through you** – The conversation ends not with a canned close, but with the client saying yes to themselves and to the roadmap to transformation we have laid in front of them.

Doesn't this feel better what you thought sales would involve? See Fig. 25 for a summary of the Old versus New Sales Model.

FIG. 25 - OLD VS. NEW SALES MODEL

Old Model	New Model
Cold calling	Warm leads
Competitive, scarcity-based	Cooperative, abundance-based
Aggressive, disrespectful	Authentic, respectful
Bait and switch	Lead with value
Overcome objections	Answer questions
Close the sale	Enroll/invite

PREPARING FOR THE CALL

Whether you're meeting with the prospect in person or by phone or video conference, you will need to prepare yourself for each call, mentally and energetically. First, get into the spirit of service mentioned above. One way that helps do this for many experts is writing a list of things you are grateful for in that very moment, including the opportunity to serve this prospect.

To avoid getting too formal, imagine (if you are having a phone or video meeting) that you're having coffee with them to discuss their challenges so you can diagnose the problem and propose a solution. Visualize them saying yes to working with you, if it is for the highest good of both of you. You might pray to God or your angels or guides to give you a sign as to whether this is a divinely matched client for you.

Managing your energy, especially if you have several discovery calls in one day, can be challenging. Be sure you have some practices that will help renew your energy if you feel yourself starting to get tired or stale. That might include dancing, listening to some upbeat music, taking a walk, petting your dog, singing, or simply doing some breath work. Many of us fail to move our bodies and breathe sufficiently throughout the day, so simply reminding ourselves to do that will help keep our energy up.

Also, keep in mind that your role in this conversation is not so much one of a leader, but rather a tour guide. You are helping the client discover the true essence of their problem, which is actually worse than they thought. It might be a long-standing issue, or they just may not have realized what they didn't know. Hold space for them to make that discovery and grab on to your solution like a life preserver.

THE CONSCIOUS CONVERSATIONS
TO CLIENTS ROADMAP

Figure 26 illustrates the six primary parts of the Conscious Conversations to Clients' Roadmap.

FIG. 26 - CONSCIOUS CONVERSATIONS TO CLIENTS ROADMAP

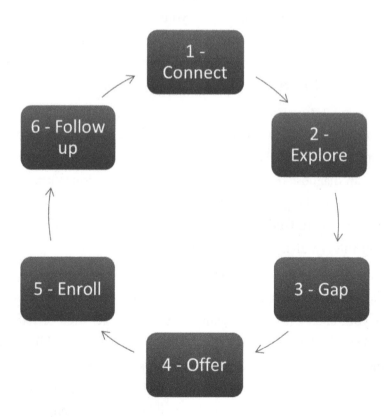

Each of the six phases of the conversation has several parts to it. Let's walk through it step-by-step.

PHASE 1: CONNECT

Sometimes, if you already met the person at a networking event or somewhere else, your connection with them will be established by simply reminding each other of the connection. You might say, "It was so great meeting you at the XYZ event last week." If you haven't met them before – for example, if they came to you through your website or a Facebook ad – begin the conversation by finding something in common. You might ask where they live and comment on any connection you have to that area. You might ask where they work and see if you have any common background. Or if you have had them complete a questionnaire prior to the call, you can refer to any of the information there that will help build rapport. Take a few minutes with this, because part of your objective with the call is for them to know, like, and trust you. The way you begin the call helps begin that process.

The second part of phase 1 is to set expectations for the call. You will want to let them know how long the call will be (usually 45 minutes), and that you will be exploring their goals, challenges, and if or how your services might be able to help them. If it seems like there's a fit, we can discuss the possibility of working together at the end. Ask them if that makes sense to them.

PHASE 2: EXPLORE

Once you've established rapport with the prospect, now you want to gain some insight into why they sought you out in the first place. Ask some questions to find out more about their current life situation.

- Where do they work? Do they enjoy it?
- Are they married?
- Is their spouse supportive of the change they want to make?

- Do they have children? Find out more about those children and whether they have any special requirements financially or emotionally of the prospect.
- If it is relevant, ask them how much they are earning or making in their business, and whether it is sufficient to meet their needs.

Most Conscious Experts forget to ask these kinds of questions and then end up facing objections such as the person having to talk to their spouse, or finding out they have a child with special needs, all of which could have been revealed earlier in the call.

The second part of phase 2 is to explore the challenges they have in your area of expertise. If you are a health expert, you would be asking them about their weight, their fitness, and the like. If your business coach, you would be asking them many questions about their business and various aspects of it, both whether they have that aspect in place, whether it is working, and what they have already tried to get it working better.

Then, ask them to share with you the goals they have for their life and their business. Draw them out so they paint a picture of their ideal scenario, not just something like "I would be earning more money and have more freedom." Get into details – if they want to travel, where would they go? If they want more time, how will they spend that time? If they want more money, what would be some of the things they would want to buy? You want to help them tap into the excitement that can come once they have the solution that you offer.

PHASE 3: GAP

Now that you have helped your prospect clarify what they want, as well as the challenges they have been having in obtaining it, summarize the gap between the two as they have explained it to you. Reflect back the concerns you heard them share, what they want, and what is lacking - whether that be a plan, money, time, or resources. Which of the steps in your Conscious Signature System is their greatest need now? Confirm that is why they sought you out for the call today. And of course, if the gap is not something that aligns with your Micro–niche, it might be best to stop the call right here.

Assuming their needs and your services are a match, the second part of phase 3 is to qualify the client. This will be the first time in the conversation where you speak for a while, rather than asking them questions. Have in mind the top three traits you know are required in order for a client to be successful in working with you. These might be things like being an action taker, having a positive attitude, being committed, being resourceful, being coachable or being decisive. Then, for each of those traits, ask them how they would rate themselves on a scale from one to ten, with ten being the highest. You are trying to determine how committed they are to get what they say they want. If they are a nine or 10, continue with the conversation. If they are in eight or less, ask them what it would take to make it at 10 before you move forward.

Next, ask them if they would like you to share with them how you could help them realize their ideal lifestyle or business. Most of the time, the prospect will say yes. But this way you have their permission before you begin to explain how your services work. Express your confidence in the fact that you can help them solve their problem.

PHASE 4: OFFER

With their permission, take a few minutes to describe how your services work, focusing on what it means to them and how it benefits them. Emphasize that it is a transformational process that has been proven – whether through your own experience or a combination of your experience and that of your clients. Don't rush this, and be sure you focus on the benefits, not just features. Benefits are what they get from your services; features are how it is delivered.

Also, point out that to be successful in the program, they must possess the three traits you just described. Ask them if that is what they are going to do.

If you have more than one level of services, such as the silver, gold, and platinum level, describe how they differ, and make a recommendation based on what you have learned about the prospect. Ask them how that sounds to them.

Notice we have not discussed anything about pricing yet. Ask them if they would like to discuss the investment (and I always call it an investment, not cost or price, because the expectation is that they will get a return on that investment and your language will influence how they think about it).

Assuming they want to hear about the investment, tell them what the normal price would be (which is more than you will be asking them to pay). Then, you can offer them what is called a Fast Action Discount, or Fast Action Scholarship, by saying that for those who are ready to change their situation immediately, you will take care of the first X amount so that what they would invest today is Y (e.g. normal price is $10,000, you might offer of fast action discount of $4000 off that, so that it is a net of $6000 paid in full today).

Then, STOP. Don't offer payment plans and don't ask if they can afford it – say nothing. Wait for them to respond. They will! And many times they will knock your socks off by saying, "Okay, let's do it." Being the one to talk first can cause you to get defensive – and you don't need to do that in the Conscious Conversations to Clients model.

PHASE 5: ENROLL

If they don't move ahead to payment and say yes when you first describe the investment, move to the section below on Dealing with Objections/ Questions. This is the point where you would offer them a payment plan if money is the only obstacle they have – or become a consultant and brainstorm with them about where they could come up with the money if they don't have it readily available.

Once you successfully answer their questions and they are ready to enroll, **take their payment information immediately.** If possible, avoid sending them a link or letting them finish what they are doing now to complete the investment. As a practical matter, your chances of them actually following through to enroll diminish substantially as soon as they hang up the phone. The fact of the matter is that emotionally they are ready to invest now, so follow through on that momentum. Remember our metaphor of finding that great outfit at the mall? What if you found the outfit, tried it on, and loved it - but left it at the store and then went shopping at different stores. Isn't it likely that you'd drive on home without going back to get the outfit you loved? This same dynamic applies when having a conversation with a prospect about your services.

Once payment is complete, your next step is to congratulate them. "You've made a great investment, we're going to do some amazing work together."

Then, explain what will happen next. Will they get an email, a package in the mail, a call from a staff member? When do they start, how do they schedule etc.

PHASE 6 – FOLLOW-UP

Finally, be sure you thank them and follow up in another way, after the call. This is called a "stick" strategy, and helps stave off any client feelings of "buyer's remorse" or "what did I just do?". Give them an initial intake form or assessment to complete, provide an introductory or orientation module to watch, and/or send them a small gift, such as a journal or other memento appropriate to your services. Then, WOW the client in your delivery, as we discuss in the next chapter and they'll keep coming back for more.

BEST WAYS TO OVERCOME "OBJECTIONS" (AKA QUESTIONS)

The very best way to handle objections is not to have them come up. By asking questions like, "is there anything else?" and "what other goals/challenges are you facing?" along the way in the call, you can address any issues then, instead of at the end. You're in a sense "closing the chapter" on each issue through each phase of the conversation so you enter the next "chapter" with a clear agenda.

In the old sales model, you would wait till the end to "close" the sale. By contrast, in Conscious Conversations to Clients, you recognize that the enrollment begins when the call begins. It's a process that goes on throughout the 45 minutes or so of the discovery call. It ends with them saying "yes" and giving you their payment information.

An "objection" is simply a question remaining in the prospect's mind that means they are not ready to buy yet. And if you do a great job of closing the chapters along the way, you may find there are a few remaining questions at the end.

COMMON "OBJECTIONS"

By far the most common objections are:

(1) I don't have the money.

(2) I have to ask my spouse/angels/banker before I can commit.

(1) Money Objection

I always remind myself – and my prospects – that anyone can find the money for something they really want. If your favorite musical performer decided to make a tour stop in your city unexpectedly in three days, and tickets were $200, would you find a way to go, even if it meant tapping your "rainy day fund" or going without something else?

Similarly, if you have sufficiently amplified your prospect's problem and helped them feel the gap between that and their ideal state of being, they will feel an urgency to get a solution – your solution. Using the Fast Action Discount, good only while you are on the call, helps create additional urgency.

When dealing with the money issue, this can be a helpful response:

- "If we take [money] off the table, is there any other reason you wouldn't move forward?" If they won't, they aren't really saying yes.

- If they say no, then become a consultant and help them solve the money issue. Provide resources such as lending sources for investors and small business owners and/or brainstorm what they could sell, do without temporarily or cash in (401k, IRA, home equity line of credit). Embody your service mindset. Also affirm with them that, as Raymond Holliwell says in *Working with the Law*, "No desire can be felt until the supply is ready to appear." The money IS available – they just need to expect it and intend to manifest it.

- Give them a specific time to raise the money, knowing that once they get off the call with you, the investment goes up to the normal price (i.e., the Fast Action Discount expires).

(2) Talk to My Spouse/Angels/Bank Objection

It is quite common to use this objection as a delay tactic so that the prospect does not have to face their fear of actually changing their familiar habits or patterns. They don't do this consciously, but since feeling the fear is uncomfortable, they're looking for any way to divert their attention from it.

Remember in phase two above, you asked your prospect whether they were married or in a committed relationship and whether that person is supportive of their change. If so, refer back to that part of the conversation and ask if anything has changed. You can also ask, if it is a business investment you're selling:

- Is your spouse a partner in your business?
- Do you make all business decisions together?

Ideally you would ask these questions as part of phase two so they don't come up here.

Experience tells us that 90% of those who say they have to go away and "think about it" or consult with someone do not come back with a yes in the follow-up appointment. They use the time between appointments to talk themselves out of the investment. That's just a fact – which makes it doubly important to help them think all the way through this objection now.

If the spouse would actually be okay with them making the investment and telling the spouse afterward, you can move forward. But if they have to consult with that person or meditate on it or talk with their investment banker about transferring funds, be *very specific* about scheduling a "bookend appointment" within 24 hours. Optionally, you can collect a nonrefundable deposit to secure the Fast Action price, and then ask them:

- When can you talk with that person?
- "Let's book a session tomorrow morning – can he/she attend too? That way you won't have to try to remember all the information I shared with you today, I can explain it so they understand it too."

You may need to resell them at that point, but enroll them then, as soon as the objection is cleared.

TRAINING OTHERS TO EXPAND YOUR SALES TEAM

Since most Conscious Experts are not natural salespeople, it's easy to want to delegate this function before you should. Don't do it.

You do not want someone with a traditional sales background – perhaps using the old sales model – selling your transformational services to your Tribe. As we have seen in exploring the old versus new approach to sales, our focus is on attracting people to transformation, not just completing a transaction with them.

You should be consistently enrolling at least 10 new clients per month before you begin considering bringing another salesperson on board. In fact, your happy clients may be the best people to train to do Conscious Conversations to Clients because they have experienced your system and have seen the results firsthand.

As you hone in on your approach to get more consistent results, record your sales calls and begin to develop a step-by-step script that your trainees can use. While they won't use it word for word, it will be helpful as they bring their own perspective to their calls.

Client enrollment specialists typically get paid a commission on each client they enroll, rather than a salary or wage for time spent.

Congratulations – you've made the sale! For what come next, see the next chapter.

PART 5

DELIVERING YOUR GIFTS AND GROWING YOUR BUSINESS

CHAPTER 9

SECRET # 7: YOUR CONSCIOUS CUSTOMER CARE/CREATING THE WOW EXPERIENCE

After a normal middle-class upbringing, Leah got her degree in psychology and went to work in a university career center, helping graduates get jobs. Even though the college was somewhat relaxed in its structures, Leah brought both organization and harmony to the way she served the students.

When she was 29, Leah was headed home for spring break when the car she was riding in was hit by an 18-wheel trailer/tractor, and she was seriously wounded. In fact, when she woke from her coma she found she had a new skill: she could see auras around people. Leah was unsure what this would mean to her, but recognized it was a special gift.

She left her work at the college and searched to find a position that fulfilled her after the accident. Leah tried new leadership roles and found she either tried to move forward too fast or shied away from leadership for fear of rejection. It was difficult for her to ask for help – even when she struggled severely in her work and personal life. For years she wondered what she was truly here to do. Finally, as she entered her 40's, she realized her life's work was to share her aura-reading gifts through readings, healing sessions, and group workshops. She felt wonderful when she was doing the workshops. But the actual preparation and marketing did not come easily, and she frequently doubted herself.

Ultimately, she moved to the spiritual community of Sedona, Arizona. There, she can freely express her divine gifts doing readings at a spiritual center in that sacred vortex location, as well as facilitating workshops and offering ongoing mentorship with select clients.

WHAT YOU'LL LEARN IN THIS CHAPTER

- Chakra 7 and Its Impact
- The Chakra 7 Business type
- How to WOW Your Clients with Your Service Delivery
- How to Cultivate Tribe Champions
- Key Business Systems for Seamless Service Delivery
- How to Strategically Use Testimonials to Engage and Connect Your Tribe

THE 7ᵀᴴ CHAKRA: CROWN

WHAT THE CROWN CHAKRA FOCUSES ON

The crown chakra is located at the top of your head – right where the soft spot is on babies. Its focus is your connection with God, your Higher Power, higher consciousness and the divine in life.

When the crown chakra is clear, you are comfortable and aligned with your chosen beliefs about God, spirituality and religion. You may follow a traditional religion or find your own version of God in nature. But whatever your choice, you embrace it and feel no need to justify it to others.

In the business context, your views about God may not seem relevant – but since all aspects of your energy system are connected, wounds or disconnects can affect every area of your life, including your business. And if, like me, you view your work in the world as closely tied to your

Divine Purpose (e.g. healer, spiritual coach, life purpose coach etc.), then recognizing the invisible help you have in sharing that work is key.

HOW TO KNOW IF YOUR 7TH CHAKRA IS BLOCKED

When your crown chakra is blocked, you will feel cynical, closed-minded, and like you have to do it all (Superwoman/man Syndrome). You will not realize that a Higher Power inspires your work, and will feel disconnected from God.

And if you do not believe that a Higher Power is guiding and supporting you, you will feel overworked, get exhausted easily, and be unwilling to delegate.

The growth of your business will stall out because you are trying to do everything, or because you are focusing only on strategy and not on your energy and divine gifts.

WOUNDS THAT CAN BLOCK CHAKRA 7

Some of the earmarks of blockages at the crown chakra include early childhood religious wounds, such as overly strict discipline, prohibiting certain foods or activities. Being forced to attend church several times a week, or being forced to go when you didn't want to can also form wounds. Other wounds can come from growing up trained to be entirely self-sufficient, which in turn can lead to an atheistic outlook and a refusal to depend on anything outside yourself.

If a parent or family member abandoned you and you had to support yourself early in life, you may conclude that God has abandoned you too. Other tragedies such as an illness or the untimely death of a child may lead you to feel God has abandoned you. It often takes another highly emotional issue or deep inner work to find your way back to a God with which you feel comfortable.

THE CHAKRA 7 BUSINESS TYPE

Chakra Business Type 7, Connector, is a business that helps people connect more deeply to their concept of God, the Universe or the Divine. It may also help people heal religious wounds from childhood, as well as anger or resentment toward God or feelings of separation stemming from a past tragedy.

Examples include healers, some ministers, therapists, grief coaches and more.

CHAKRA 7 CLEARING & ACTIVATION

See marciabench.com/cca-book-resources for the chakra clearing and activation for your 7th chakra.

CHAKRA 7 CREATION LAW: THE LAW OF INCREASE

There is a principle in manifesting, "That which you focus on multiplies." So if you are constantly thinking about lack, about how you never get what you want, and about how bad the world is, the more the world will show up that way for you. And conversely, if you give thanks for every new client, every dollar that comes in, and every new opportunity – and you focus on your vision coming into physical form – then you will experience more of that too!

What we focus our attention on is pivotal, both in initially *attracting* anything, any person or any situation – as well as in *increasing* the amount of it that we have in our lives.

A key practice that activates the Law of Increase is gratitude. In his book *Working with the Law*, Raymond Holliwell points out:, "When we praise the richness and opulence of God, the Law, our thoughts are greatly increased in the mental atmosphere. This increase affects our being in that it reflects in everything our mind and hands may touch...[On the other hand,] if we are contracting our thought through fear, criticism, and complaint, we reflect that contraction and our results are delayed or frozen."

Therefore, when you reach a place in your business that is characterized more by lack than abundance, consider whether you have been allowing in thoughts of fear, criticism or complaint. That can be the beginning of a downward spiral culminating in lack!

In *Manifesting Your Destiny*, Dr. Wayne Dyer offers these suggestions for cultivating gratitude.

1. See yourself as a recipient, not a victim.

2. Silently express gratitude when you see your desires manifesting.

3. Tell those around you how much you appreciate them.

4. Be thankful and avoid complaining.

5. Begin each day with gratitude.

6. Be grateful for the suffering and struggles in your life.

He continues, "Remember, it is the nature of thoughts to increase. The more your thoughts are centered on what is missing, the more deficient you feel and the more complaints you will utter. Similarly, the more you practice gratitude, the more you are thankful and appreciative of all that life provides, the more you feed your experience of abundance and love."

BUSINESS TASKS ASSOCIATED WITH CHAKRA 7

So what business tasks are associated with the 7th chakra?

- How to WOW Your Clients with Your Service Delivery
- How to Cultivate Tribe Champions
- Key Business Systems For Seamless Service Delivery
- How to Strategically Use Testimonials To Engage And Connect Your Tribe

Let's discuss each in turn.

HOW TO WOW YOUR CLIENTS WITH YOUR SERVICE DELIVERY

Woo hoo – your new client enrolled! You can relax now, right?

No, your work hasn't ended – it has just begun.

Your client hired you because you have created a unique movement, Tribe, and services package perfectly suited to their needs. Now that they have said yes, your job is to continue their experience of being drawn to you – and loving their experience - as they receive your services.

That means WOWing them by going above and beyond what they expected – under-promising and over-delivering, all without compromising your own healthy boundaries and desired lifestyle. This leads to exceptional client results and cultivates raving fans.

WHY WOW YOUR CLIENTS

Here are the reasons why it's key to WOW your clients today:

- Conscious sales means continuing the positive experience and keeping your promises once they have invested.
- Exceptional customer service and service delivery sets you apart – in a good way – from your Related Providers because it is rare.
- WOW service gives you legitimacy in a world of online business suspicion.
- You'll keep them coming back and ascending to higher levels of engagement and work with you.
- WOW service leads to a stream of quality referrals to new clients.

WOW CLIENT SERVICE IDEAS AND TIPS

So how do you WOW your clients as they go through your course, coaching program, healing process or live event?

- **Be prompt!** I can't tell you how many times, during the course of a month, I receive compliments from prospects and clients telling me how grateful they are for our prompt response. It seems to be a lost art. Though we are a digital society, too many people and businesses hide behind excuses, procrastination and delays, as reasons not to keep promises or show up on time. And so, simply keeping your promises as to what you will deliver and when gives you a clear advantage.

- **Establish clear expectations.** Clearly communicate – verbally and in writing – with your client exactly what will happen, how the process will work and key timelines. This not only ensures that both of you are on the same page, but avoids misunderstandings later on if the client was expecting one thing and you're delivering something else. We all listen through the filters of our past experience, so clear communication is key.

- **Surprise them!** Give them an onboarding gift or a bonus they aren't expecting. While you may have fast action bonuses for those who enroll first, you may also want to arrange a special acknowledgment for new clients, attendees, or purchasers, such as a gift card to a coffee shop or online store, or branded collateral, such as a calendar, mouse pad, or other useful item that will keep your name in front of them.

- **Respond quickly to questions and concerns.** If, on top of feeling confused or uncertain about something, a client doesn't get a prompt answer to a question, problems can quickly escalate. Either you or a client relations team member should have a system in place to respond within one business day of all technical and substantive questions. Some people use a support ticket software for this once volume is sufficient to justify it.

- **Call on their expertise if it adds to the class or coaching experience.** Sometimes you will attract a client or student into your programs that has significant training or experience in the exact area you're teaching or coaching about. Don't be intimidated –

instead, embrace it and use it to enrich the experience for everyone. Ask them for their thoughts on certain key points. Once they start asking questions of you, you'll know they are engaged.

HOW TO CULTIVATE TRIBE CHAMPIONS

Over time you will notice there are a few of your Tribe members who have significant breakthroughs and great results. They become evangelists or champions of your work. One way of cultivating these champions is to do great work that helps people get amazing results. The reason we want to cultivate champions or evangelists within our Tribe is that they are often very positive, action-taking people who will invite others like themselves to your work. These are ideal clients.

But we need to do more than just recognize that they are there – we want to nurture them, reward them, and encourage them to continue their relationship with us. Some of the ways that we can do that include:

- Feature their success stories on your webpages and in your website – see more on that below.

- Feature them as case studies in your newsletter.

- Invite them to share their story from the stage in your seminars, workshops, or live multi-day events.

- Whenever they refer someone to you, compensate them with anything from a complementary session to an Amazon gift card, to flowers or tickets to their favorite event or game - or a more expensive item depending on the size of the business that resulted from the referral.

- Host special gatherings just for these champions – for example, you could have a private happy hour in a hospitality suite the day before your live multi-day event.

The sky is the limit - but the point is that you want to express your gratitude to them for their patronage and the referrals so that, according to the Law of Increase, they will enthusiastically want to continue and bring you more business in future.

KEY BUSINESS SYSTEMS FOR SEAMLESS SERVICE DELIVERY

One of the biggest traps I see new Conscious Experts falling into is trying to master every piece of software they will need for their business instead of hiring part-time virtual help already familiar with the software systems needed.

As the CEO of your expert business, your job is to provide direction and focus for both overall business strategy and the results that will lead to the fulfillment of that strategy. This naturally includes engaging other people to handle those tasks that are below your billable rate.

While you need to understand, in a big picture sense, what software and systems you need, you do not need to be the one inputting to them. And, if you have the right kind of virtual help, they will be suggesting new options to you as technology rapidly changes.

See separate Business Systems Checklist marciabench.com/cca-book-resources for more details.

You will need various systems in six key areas, as illustrated in Fig. 27:

1. Document handling
2. Scheduling
3. Bookkeeping
4. Website
5. Marketing
6. Team

FIG. 27 - 6 KINDS OF BUSINESS SYSTEMS

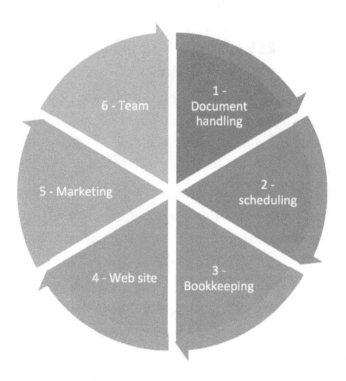

1. **Document handling** – your business will require that you create documents in word processing software, spreadsheets, slides for presentations, and the like, as well as make those available securely to team members with whom you are working. The Microsoft Office suite for PC users works great for this, and the Mac programs Pages, Numbers and Keynote perform that function for Mac users. Document sharing and storage can be done through Google Docs, Dropbox, or a similar cloud-based system. You may wish to use Evernote to populate your content across various devices, Adobesign for electronic document signing, lastpass.com to store your passwords, and topic-based folders within your email program, such as Outlook. Be sure you get administrative support here.

2. **Scheduling** – while a paper calendar may serve this purpose for your personal life, once you become a business owner, an electronic calendar system for both your personal and business commitments can greatly simplify your life. If you have a virtual assistant or marketing assistant booking calls with prospects, clients, media, promotional partners or others for you, an online calendar system is essential. We recommend the free Google calendar system, particularly because it is portable, on your phone at all times, and accessible by others to whom you give permission. It also interfaces nicely with client scheduling systems such as acuityscheduling.com, meet me.so, and similar programs. Both will be necessary to avoid having to go back and forth through email in order to book a session with a client or prospect. They simply choose a time it's available on your calendar and convenient for them - and it is updated in real time.

3. **Bookkeeping** – a bookkeeper should be one of the first people that you hire to help you on a part-time basis. However, you will need to have ways of spot-checking your income and expenses as well as providing reports to you weekly, monthly, quarterly, and upon request. The most flexible system for most Conscious Experts is QuickBooks online. My bookkeeper is not in the same city or state where I live, but yet can access those records remotely and run payroll, as well as through that site. Another helpful software in the area of bookkeeping is shoebox.com to manage your receipts so they can be provided to your bookkeeper and CPA.

4. **Web site** – when you get to the point where you need a website for your business, one of the first things you will need is a design platform. The most universally used and search engine friendly is Word Press.com. Within that you will need to choose a theme, we recommend you talk with your web designer regarding that. That website will in turn that need to be hosted on the Internet so that it has an address or URL. We recommend hostmonster.com or blue-host.com for this purpose.

Before you have a full website, you can often get by with a simple opt-in page created in either leadpages.net or clickfunnels.com. You will need those sites later to promote various specific kinds of classes, products, events, coaching programs, and other offerings.

In order for clients to purchase from you, you will need several tools that talk with each other, including a credit card processor, such as a reseller of authorize.net. The following link on their website explains this process in a short video: https://www.authorize.net/resources/howitworksdiagram/.

To create the payment links themselves, you will need either a shopping cart program, such as a smartcart.com or 1shoppingcart.com, or a business account at Paypal.com.

5. **Marketing** – the fifth category of business tools that you will need relates to your marketing. As people opt in to your free resources on the pages you create on leadpages.net or clickfunnels.com, you will be gathering names and email addresses for follow-up. Storing these in a secure, CANSPAM-compliant service is very critical to your ongoing marketing. Both leadpages and Clickfunnels have such a service as an option. We recommend aweber.com, constantcontact.com or getresponse.com for the new business. As your business and list grows, you can move up to Infusionsoft.com or ontraport.com. Also, in order to host webinars and provide live or recorded class content for your clients or students, you will need to use zoom.us or a similar program for webinars. Later, when you automate your webinar, you will also need stealthseminars.com.

6. **Team** - finally, as you begin to use virtual assistants and other virtual staff, you will need to coordinate their efforts. For project and team management, asana.com, teamwork.com, or basecamp.com are useful. Team members can keep track of their hours on myhours.com so you can spot-check the hours of each team member throughout the month. Sweetprocess.com is helpful for creation

and updating of company policies so everyone is on the same page with regard to those. And finally, podio.com or a similar software can store all information related to each of your clients, students, and or members, including details down to their contact and credit card information, the programs they have purchased, and more.

HOW TO STRATEGICALLY USE TESTIMONIALS TO ENGAGE AND CONNECT YOUR TRIBE

Now that we have reached the seventh step of Conscious Client Attraction, your clients or students may have begun to create their own programs and enroll their own clients and students into them. Therefore, there should be some results that you can begin to identify and share. Your clients may not spontaneously pass these on to you. You need to be paying attention to what they say in classes and coaching sessions, what you observe when the breakthroughs happen in your live workshops and events, as well as what they share on social media.

Then, acknowledge their accomplishment and help them convert it into a testimonial that you can use in promoting your future programs. They may need your help in wording it. I often provide a draft for my clients to get them started. Today, one of the best ways to use testimonials is to have them do it on a short video on Facebook or YouTube. You can either use it as is by downloading it, or have it transcribed and use the print version as well.

Why is it so important to elicit testimonials? Isn't your story enough to sell your brand/services?

Well, yes and no! Your story is definitely important and needs to be told. But client stories provide validation and credibility that you have helped others get their own results too. These stories show that the prospect doesn't need to be you (with whatever advantages they believe you have) to succeed.

WHAT TO INCLUDE IN A TESTIMONIAL

The most powerful testimonials are more than just compliments on how wonderful you are at what you do – they showcase *specific results* the client has obtained through your programs or mentoring.

Contrast:

"Jane is such a great coach. I felt totally comfortable with her and she helped me a lot. I recommend her."

Versus:

"Through working with Jane, I overcame my previously unknown, lifelong fear of wealth and have just bought my first rental house. My family will be secure for the long term now."

See the difference?

You'll probably need to ask your clients some questions to fill in their story.

- What was your "before" situation? What were you doing? What wasn't working? How were you feeling?

- Then, as a result of the work they did with you, what strategies did you implement? What specific results did you obtain? What is the ripple effect of these results in your family, their fitness, their friendships, their faith and their finances?

- Draw out the full "after" story and key takeaways – then you can shorten it to the nuggets you want to use in specific situations.

Once you get the details needed to tell their story, be sure you obtain permission, through a Release document, to share their full name and photograph on your marketing materials and website. However, we recommend that you don't directly link to your client's website when you publish their testimonial. List it if desired, but don't hyperlink to it – keep them on your page!

EXAMPLE:

"Marcia, I am so grateful to have found your career coach training and your Conscious Client Attraction mentoring to guide me. You have been a tremendous help to me in growing my business and teaching me the parts of business I needed to learn. Thanks to your help, my business is on the fast track to success. **I enrolled 14 new career-coaching clients and 2 retainer clients in the last 7 weeks, and my income has doubled since I started your Conscious Client Attraction Blueprint program.** I am on track to achieve my Big Goal for the year now – all thanks to you!"

—*Melissa Beaudet, Career Coach Experts*

HOW TO USE TESTIMONIALS

You can use these testimonials in countless ways. The only limitations are those established by the Federal Trade Commission such as the requirement that you not use an endorsement of one program or service to promote another one that that person has not personally experienced. See the FTC website for additional relevant guidelines.

Here are some ideas as to where you might use your client testimonials:

- Have a "client love" or "success stories" page on your website – see our sites for examples.

- Integrate them into the body and at the end of your sales pages promoting classes, coaching, membership programs etc.

- Use in emails when marketing your services.

- Post them around the room in your workshop space.

- Have slides created that show in between sessions at a live event of your featured clients and their results.

Now that we have progressed all the way through the primary chakra system from the lower spine to the top of the head, it's now time to look at ways to scale our businesses and activate all of the energy centers fully so that your message and movement are globally recognized and constantly expanding.

CHAPTER 10

SECRET # 8: YOUR CONSCIOUS BUSINESS/ MOVEMENT EXPANSION & GROWTH

"I was born and grew up in Bulgaria, a small country in southeastern Europe, where connection to God was forbidden by law. In 1986, I moved to Germany, where, in 1991, I was blessed to open my own dental practice.

"Back then I thought I was on top of the world having my own practice in a foreign country. But I came to realize that as a dentist, I was limited in my ability to serve people. Patients came to me not to get the holes in their teeth fixed, but rather desired to get the holes in their lives healed. And I could not do this as a dentist. I was not happy at all.

"In that profession I had to work eight or nine hours a day and have five to ten employees in my dental office. I worked very hard to build a successful business and was earning $100,000. But in my country, of that income, 55% comes off the top for your team. Then you have to pay your taxes, which are significant. That doesn't leave much net revenue for the business owner.

"After several years of practice, I was diagnosed with uterine cancer. I had to have surgery, and the first surgery didn't work. Then they had to perform a second one. And I am very grateful to be alive 20 years after the surgery, and thriving not just surviving. As a cancer survivor, I wanted to help cancer patients with their healing. I attracted a few clients, but not enough to sustain myself.

"I dabbled in several other things, including a new model for dentistry, a bed and breakfast, and translation services. In 2011, I faced bankruptcy. And then the bankruptcy lawyer sold my dental office, which was a great opportunity for me. I call it being catapulted by life to where I was supposed to be. So one day I sat down and asked the Divine, 'What do you really want me to do?' The answer started to come.

"A few months later, I was, invited to a community where I could present on a telesummit. After being introduced to the host's community of 20,000 people and presenting there, 360 people bought the packages she was offering. That package included a healing program I created. Wow! Things took off from there.

"Now I'm working with people giving them hour-long sessions, where they tell me what their problem is, and I pray to the Divine to provide transformation for them and get guidance. And it seems to work very well. One 68-year-old woman who hadn't been able to walk for 16 years put down her walker after a session, and has been able to walk ever since.

"I'm actually earning more now doing spiritual work than I did as a dentist – without the stress and the team. This was my dream. It feels right to me. Now, I work for maybe five hours per day and have freedom, flexibility and so much more. I'm a very happy grandma of a 3-year-old boy and grateful to get to spend time with him. I have found my voice and my ideal life – the best of all worlds."

— *Dr. Madlena Kantscheff*

WHAT YOU'LL LEARN IN THIS CHAPTER

- Chakra 8 and Its Impact
- The Chakra 8 Business Type
- The Creation Law of Unity

- How to Delegate Strategically from The Start
- How to Overcome the Upper Limits Problem
- How to Scale Your Business and "Clone" Yourself

CHAKRA 8: AURA

WHAT THE AURA CHAKRA FOCUSES ON

The aura chakra encases your physical body in energy, going four feet out in all directions. It focuses on being the Light, your oneness with God, aka the Universe, and wholeness. Its colors change based on how clear the rest of your chakras are. Many people think of it as a protective energetic layer around you, which it is. But it is also a field through which you radiate your essence. If you've ever stood next to someone you just met and felt like you could pick up on what he or she was thinking and feeling, you were likely perceiving their aura.

When your aura is clear white, it is an indication of spiritual and energetic health and an absence of blockages in your other chakras. You will feel spiritually integrated within yourself and able to connect with others.

In the business context, your aura has to do with how people experience you and your energy, both virtually and in person. We are all energetic beings. Whether we are aware of it or not, we move towards or away from someone based on their energy. Since the Conscious Client Attraction model is based on attraction, it is critical you keep your aura as clear as possible. This is one of the reasons we asked you to put your money karma drama outside the door when you're in a sales conversation or writing marketing copy. Your neediness, desperation or fear can come through energetically in a conversation, even if you think you have stopped focusing on it. Your aura has everything to do with how quickly you can grow your business. What we call charisma is directly related to having a clear aura as well. People are irresistibly drawn to the clarity and confidence that comes from a clear aura.

At this stage in your business development, you will need to let go of the belief that no one can do it like you can. While that may be true when it comes to your presentations, your coaching or other service delivery, it is not true in other aspects of your business. The most successful CEOs surround themselves with people who are more talented than they are in that person's specific area of expertise. Thus, "a rising tide floats all boats" – the combined high-level of expertise in all areas of your business will elevate the scope of your transformational impact exponentially faster than by trying to do everything yourself.

HOW TO KNOW IF YOUR 8TH CHAKRA IS BLOCKED

If your aura is blocked, you will notice that you feel separated from others, from God, and from yourself. You may be so traumatized by a past life event that you cannot release the energy. That in turn clouds your aura.

You may fear that your success is "too good to be true" – and insist on staying in control. You won't ask for help in your business or in setting up systems.

You may be holding onto resentments or other issues that draw energy from the current moment, affecting not only the chakra connected to that issue, but your aura as well.

WOUNDS THAT CAN BLOCK CHAKRA 8

One kind of events that can causes wounds at the aura chakra include being ridiculed or belittled repeatedly by a parent or authority figure, leaving you to believe you are worthless.

Religious persecution or disillusionment can cause an aura wound if it is not healed. I shared with you earlier my turning point in college, when I was no longer comfortable with my childhood beliefs. I lost my best friends, and my parents and I did not speak for a full year, partly based on this decision to change religions. Had I not been able to fully integrate into a broader way of thinking, that wound could still be affecting my aura chakra today.

Another type of aura wound stems from a traumatic breakup of a primary relationship, especially if it involves deceit or unfaithfulness, where you are unwilling or unable to forgive that person.

Sudden death of a loved one, especially if it was murder or otherwise at the hands of a person who you believe wronged you, can deeply affect your aura, especially if you are unwilling or unable to forgive them.

A final category of wounds is feeling like God abandoned you because of one of these types of traumatic incidents or because you feel like life dealt you a bad hand of cards.

Clearly, these are significant wounds that usually cannot be healed by simply chanting a few affirmations. They are more complex than other chakra wounds because each or wound is tied to another chakra and intertwined with its energy. If you feel like your aura is blocked or cloudy, you might consider having an aura photograph taken or going to an intuitive that can perceive your aura to better locate the source of the wound if you do not know.

THE CHAKRA 8 BUSINESS TYPE

Chakra Business Type 8, Oneness, is a business that helps people embody oneness with humanity, God and creation. It may also help people heal wounds at other chakras that cause disruption in their aura.

Examples include spiritual healers, ministers, spiritual practitioners, and spiritual coaches.

CHAKRA 8 CLEARING & ACTIVATION

See marciabench.com/cca-book-resources for the chakra clearing and activation for your 8th chakra.

CHAKRA 8 CREATION LAW: THE LAW OF UNITY

Living on the planet that we do, it appears that each one of us is a separate entity. Black and white, right and wrong - duality is our daily experience.

But as we grow spiritually and evolve in our businesses, we begin to realize the truth: each of us and everything around us is part of one amazing unified field. The separation we perceive is but an illusion.

It always makes me shake my head when I am in the midst of grappling with an issue, and then when I dial into a coaching session with a client I find that they have the very same issue and are asking for my guidance in how to get through it. Was that a coincidence? I think not.

Even as I am writing this manuscript and preparing for my mother's memorial service in a few days, it has been amazing to see how many people have been brought across my path who are losing loved ones as well.

You can chalk it up to the law of attraction, and that is part of the explanation. But as experts like Dr. Fred Alan Wolf, Gregg Braden and many scientists in the quantum physics arena have discovered, everything in the universe is connected. And that doesn't just go for people – some of the most fascinating experiments I've seen are Masaru Emoto's Messages from Water. In his experiments, he showed letters to water crystals, showed pictures to them, played music to them, and prayed to them. The startling results of the frozen water crystals, under these different conditions, take your breath away. (See www.masaru-emoto.net/english/water-crystal.html)

Our thoughts, intentions, words, and actions have a ripple effect on a much wider sphere than we might expect. Imagine what this means for the transformational work we are doing in the world. There are a certain number of people we interact with individually or in groups that we know will benefit from our message. But there may be thousands or millions of others indirectly affected through the families of those we have touched personally as well as through the vibration we have set in motion.

Once we recognize this, we realize there is no "us" or "them," there is only one. When we are hurt by someone, disagree with someone, or feel jealous of another, they're simply out-picturing a part of ourselves for us to examine. The same is true when we love someone, passionately agree with someone, or feel an affinity with a person.

The other realization that comes with the Law of Unity is that there is really no limit to the impact we can have. The only obstacle in our way is the one we put in our way. In this chapter we will help you expand your vision so you become as large a force to be reckoned with as you want to be in leaving your legacy on the planet.

BUSINESS TASKS ASSOCIATED WITH CHAKRA 8

The following business tasks are associated with the aura chakra:

- How to Delegate Strategically from the Start
- How to Scale Your Business and "Clone" Yourself
- How to Overcome the Upper Limits Problem

HOW TO DELEGATE STRATEGICALLY FROM THE START

WHY DELEGATE

The one mistake that holds more Conscious Experts back than anything else, in my experience, is not hiring talent to support them, especially in administrative and software areas of their business. I love what my colleague John Assaraf says on this topic, "Hire people who play at what you have to work at."

We have been given different gifts and talents for a reason. Those of us who are called to be Conscious Experts are the minority, not the majority. Most people prefer to stay in the background and play a role that suits their talents, not be the one out front "taking the punches" and leading the way.

And thanks to the converging trends we discussed in the opening of the book – consciousness, entrepreneurship and purpose – an entire industry of support personnel for people like us has now emerged. We no longer need to hire a secretary full-time to work in our physical office – virtual part-time assistants are now readily available to work on contract performing all kinds of different functions.

WHEN TO DELEGATE/HIRE

When should you begin hiring virtual staff members and delegating what needs to be done in your business? The answer is, as soon as possible. Once you have your basic concepts and messages in place, and you have attracted your first five clients, you are probably ready for a virtual assistant. It might only be for five hours a month at first – that is how I started when I hired my first V.A. within 90 days of founding Career Coach Institute. I had years of experience as an administrative assistant myself, so many of the tasks that the typical expert would not be able to do, I could. But that was the bad news – I needed to get in the habit, as you do too, of inviting people to support and help me from the beginning. That way, I stayed in my zone of genius, as well as my pay grade!

When you consider the possibility of doing your own bookkeeping, how do you feel about that? Most Conscious Experts would rather have a root canal than do their own bookkeeping. So consider that the energy you bring to the tasks you do is key, as well as the frustration that can result when you try to master something isn't your natural talent. There are people who love to do bookkeeping, database creation, and copy writing. Let them shine! One key to scaling your business is bringing in great people with skillsets the compliment yours and creating a highly motivated team to carry your movement to the next level.

HOW TO AFFORD YOUR TEAM

Of course, hiring talent costs money. That is the primary reason most new business owners in our industry don't do it – or at least don't do it soon enough. It's very difficult to hire and train a team when you have grown to the point where things are crazy busy. You will have little patience or time to train them or orient them to your company's mission and vision. It's better to start by grooming a few specialists with a few hours, and then let the demand ebb and flow naturally. This will create a group of people that can grow with you and your business.

Being able to afford your team is not that difficult. You know from chapter 6 what your hourly billing rate would be if you were billing by the hour. What would happen if you eliminated any tasks in your business that could not be billed out at that rate? When I help Conscious Experts do this, their businesses explode.

Virtual assistants and bookkeepers vary widely in their fee structure and billable rates, but I can guarantee you their rates are significantly less than yours. For example, let's say you hire a V.A. to handle your routine email, help with scheduling your clients, and create handouts for your group program. You pay him/her $35 an hour to do that, and it might take him/her 10 hours a month. So it would cost you $350 ($35 x 10). What would you be able to do in that same amount of time? And what is 10 hours of your time worth? (Really, the comparison is with how many hours it would take you to do the same tasks that he/she could do in ten hours, and how many billable hours that takes away from your month.)

However, for this delegation formula to work, you must be sure you spend the hours you have delegated to him/her for what we call RGA's – Revenue Generating Activities. Those are normally the higher-level tasks, such as serving clients, holding enrollment conversations, and marketing activities, as well as planning the strategy and direction for your company. Anything else should be delegated.

WHAT TO DELEGATE

Once you have decided that you will bring in some help, what should you delegate? You have a general idea from our discussion about it. But keep in mind there are three types of tasks in your business, as illustrated in Fig. 28:

FIG. 28 - PYRAMID OF 3 TYPES OF TASKS

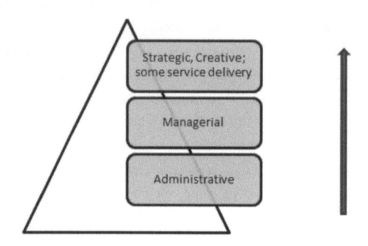

1. **Administrative** – This is the lowest level of tasks, but nevertheless key to your business. It includes such things as document preparation, correspondence, routine email, spreadsheet creation, reporting, bookkeeping, slide deck creation, client support, calendaring, social media posts, video editing and the like. This is the first area you should delegate. Choose virtual staff members who already have a level of proficiency in the type of tasks you need to get done. Some will be more comfortable with marketing and social media, others with bookkeeping and databases, and others with document preparation or video editing.

2. **Managerial** – After you have been delegating areas of responsibility in your business for a while, you may start to feel as I did a few years ago – like the one-armed paper hanger again, just like you did when you started delegating. You're delegating, but a disproportionate amount of your time gets spent managing those you have delegated, which puts most Conscious Experts outside their zone

of genius. At this point, an Online Business Manager ("OBM") can be a great help to provide the oversight of your contracted virtual team so you can concentrate on your RGA's. My colleague Tina Forsyth has an amazing training program and cadre of OBM's at her website, onlinebusinessmanager.com. You may also be able to find one through referrals or graduate one of your virtual assistants to this position if appropriate.

3. **Strategic, Creative, Some Service Delivery** – This third level of tasks is one that you rarely delegate. This is your business, so you set the strategic direction. You are your own R & D department, receiving inspiration for and helping your team implement new offerings. Some creative models are emerging in the area of service delivery. If you are offering a mastermind program, as we described in Business Model 5, you likely have two levels of service: one in which you primarily support your clients in regular group calls, and a higher one, in which participants receive both group calls and individual time with you. When the groups are small, you can easily personally provide the individual calls with your higher end clients. However, as it grows, you will want to leverage yourself in some way. Most commonly, coaches will promote one of their clients who are getting great results with their system to facilitate the coaching calls with beginner level clients, while the primary coach works with the more advanced clients.

In other cases, coaches like Melissa choose to build a team of other professionals with complementary areas of expertise, not for support, but rather to provide a diverse array of specialty mentoring to the clients. For example, a business coach who specializes in solid business strategy might bring on a mindset coach, a Facebook ads coach, a system and software coach, and perhaps a copy-writing expert. Some of those coaches could facilitate some of the group calls and individual sessions could be available on demand or a set number of sessions for client with each of the people on the team. This isn't really delegating, but rather changing the model of service delivery. But nevertheless, it frees up your time.

PERSONAL DELEGATION

In addition to delegating administrative and managerial tasks in your business, you will want to look at other things you're currently doing in your personal life that, if you got support in that area, would enhance your level of freedom. Many experts engage a personal assistant to run errands, such as picking up mail, taking in dry cleaning, doing any needed personal banking, purchasing office supplies and the like. Other tasks like dog walking, cooking, grocery shopping, and getting you packed for travel to a convention or speaking engagement are all areas where delegation is possible.

To stimulate your ideas on possible areas to delegate, Fig. 29 outlines possible roles to be filled in your business and personal life.

FIG. 29 - POSSIBLE ROLES TO FILL

Business Tasks	
CEO (you)	Business Manager
Virtual Assistants (various specialties)	Web Designer
Social Media Manager	Video Editor
Graphic Designer	Bookkeeper
Copywriter	Online Marketing
Client Concierge	Events Manager
IT/Technology Manager	Personal Assistant
Sales	Sales Support
Product Fulfillment	App Designer
Personal Tasks	
Personal Chef	Personal Trainer
Housekeeper/maid	Dog walker
Child care	Errand runner/Gal Friday

See book resource page at marciabench.com/cca-book-resources for exercise on what to delegate now in your business.

WHERE TO FIND STAFF

The very best place to find outstanding team members is through referral. Ask your colleagues if they have a great virtual assistant or personal chef or whatever it is that you are looking for who may have additional hours available.

When you are looking for a fellow coach or professional level team member, you may want to attend events where they are speaking and approach them there.

Virtual assistant associations online, as well as upwork.com, can provide you with additional contacts by specialty. However, be sure to check the references and do your due diligence before hiring someone that has not been referred to you personally.

LEGAL MATTERS

When you bring team members on, you'll need to be sure to work with your business attorney in preparing the appropriate kind of contracts for them. After all, they will have access to your proprietary intellectual property, your mailing list, and your ways of doing business. I would hate to have you become one of the horror stories I have seen where a staff member appropriates the intellectual property of the expert they're working for and forms their own business using it.

Some of the protections you'll need to have in place include:

- Specific list of responsibilities.
- How they are to be paid – whether as a contractor or employee (most are paid as contractors, but use caution if you engage them 40 hours per week as that can result in payroll taxes and penalties) – and when invoices are due.
- Notice required for any vacation or extended absences.

- Confidentiality provisions regarding your intellectual property and an agreement not to disclose confidential information, with penalties if they do.

- A noncompete agreement, especially for professional level staff.

- How their work product is stored – preferably in a cloud-based system - so if they disappear, you still have access.

- Any other provisions required by your jurisdiction.

As mentioned earlier, we recommend Legal Shield for your business legal matters. See our resource list in the book resource page at marciabench. com/cca-book-resources for how to gain access to this coverage.

HOW TO OVERCOME THE "UPPER LIMITS PROBLEM"

As the saying goes, "What got you here will not get you there." In other words, each stage of your business will require you to evolve and grow as a person – and implement new business strategies – to allow space for the next level of growth. That may mean letting go of additional areas of responsibility in your business to team members or adding more leverage to your programs. It may also require implementing new systems to automate processes, or simply expanding your vision to see how you could serve in a greater way.

But if you are aware that something needs to shift, you may unintentionally attract a roadblock that stops the progress in its tracks. In his book *The Big Leap,* Gay Hendricks describes this as the "Upper Limits Problem," in which we unconsciously sabotage our good, just when things start to go amazingly well. It can happen in our primary relationships, our health, or our business. We find ourselves pushing against the Upper Limits of our comfort zone. Instead of being willing to go beyond it, we seemingly "accidentally" experience something like a large bill, a staff member leaving without notice or the loss of a long-time client that keeps us from focusing on the growth.

This Upper Limits Problem didn't appear out of thin air. Hendricks explains that it is based in deeply embedded patterns or beliefs that we are fundamentally flawed, will be abandoned by everyone important to us, or that success is a burden instead of an opportunity. The adult part of us is encouraging us to expand and grow, but the little child inside is scared and wants things to stay the same. It is most comfortable when we play out the old scripts that were embedded in our infancy.

To surpass our Upper Limits, we must first *recognize* the problem, and understand that no matter how much we can explain that the roadblock came from outside of us, the fact is that it is of our own making. Going within, we can comfort the small child part of us wants to stay safe. We might imagine having a conversation with it to negotiate its cooperation with our larger goals. Then, we will need to consciously open to receive more good than we have ever had - and be comfortable with it.

HOW TO SCALE YOUR BUSINESS AND "CLONE" YOURSELF

Now that you have reliable lead generation and client enrollment processes, are enrolling people into a solution you feel passionate about, and are delegating the tasks you can, it is time to position yourself for greater growth.

The mature, multiple six-figure or seven-figure Conscious Expert business includes multiple streams of income as depicted in Fig. 30:

FIG. 30 - MULTIPLE INCOME STREAMS

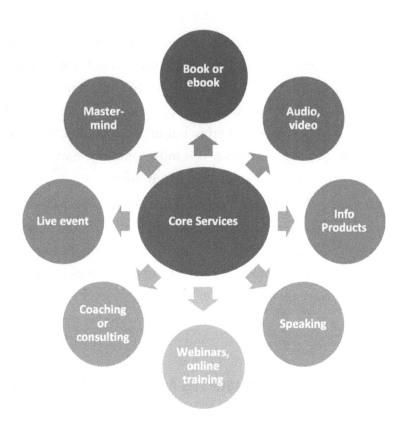

To help get you to this level, as well as grow beyond it, following are 12 strategies through which you can scale.

1. **Dramatically increase your sales/enrollments** – This strategy requires that you have structured your service delivery so you can easily accommodate a large influx of new clients, such as dripping the content through a membership portal, serving clients through group programs, or having multiple coaches on your team. With that in place, you can automate your lead generation through online ads. Those in turn lead to an automated webinar. You might provide specialized invitation-only trainings inside your Facebook group. Those leads can be sent to a team of sales team members you

have trained to enroll them. Instead of you hosting the webinars and facilitating the enrollment calls, you can automate the webinar and send leads to a team of sales team members, each talking with ten or more people per day. This way the number of clients that you enroll would grow exponentially with the growth of your team.

2. **Raise your fees** – If scaling for you refers more to income than to number of people served, then raising your fees on a regular basis can have dramatic results. If you notice sales starting to fall off when you do so, be sure you do additional mindset training with your sales team and be sure that they are not confronting their Upper Limits and keeping the increased sales from coming in. Some experts will test a level of fees until they and their team are consistently enrolling 25 to 50% of the qualified leads. Once they have enrolled a certain number at that price point, they will raise the fee by $500 or $1,000 and test to see if the conversion remains consistent.

3. **Up-level your Tribe** – Sometimes it is not what you are offering, but to whom you are offering it, that can make all the difference. There are audiences who will pay premium prices for your solution. To grow your business more quickly, focus on them. Maybe instead of all engineers, you target the senior engineers instead. Or maybe instead of all coaches, you direct your marketing messages to those who aspire to create their own global expert platform, as we do. That allows you to charge premium prices and work with more highly motivated clients.

4. **Broaden to other online portals** – Perhaps in honing your lead generation strategy, you focused primarily on Facebook ads, and those are working very well for you. Now it may be time to create and put significant energy into a YouTube channel, a LinkedIn group, a podcast, or increasing monetization in your Facebook group. Many times you can repurpose content across channels, but

each channel has its own specific guidelines to get it generating consistent leads and revenue for you.

5. **Do more interviews, podcasts, guest speaking gigs and joint ventures** – Generally speaking, your existing list of leads will only respond for a limited time to your messages. So while you want to continue communicating with them, one of the secrets to long-term success is continuing on a daily and weekly basis to add new leads to your community. One of the best ways to do this is by being featured as a guest on a podcast, a Facebook live, a guest blog post, or an interview promoted by a colleague to their list, where you can bring a complementary offering to their primary services.

6. **Shift from 1:1 to group or group to mastermind** – Whenever you start to think about scaling, go back to the five primary business models in chapter 3 and ask if you have implemented them all yet. If you are still serving clients 1:1 and your calendar is getting full, create and offer a group program. If you are doing a group program, graduate to a mastermind. The business models are there to provide a structure for you whenever you want to grow.

7. **Offer an implementation course** – Even if you have already offered a course or training a few times, your clients will pay a premium to get more of your time helping them implement what they have learned. I once took a course in the area of speaking and selling from stage. The format was simply to watch a training module before each call, and then attend weekly calls consisting of laser coaching and question-and-answer format. Each participant had ample time to get their questions answered. I paid $5,000 for that particular course, and it was well worth it.

8. **Release a book** – While direct sales from writing and selling a book is usually your smallest profit center, there is a time in the evolution of your brand when it will make sense to write one. My approach in writing this book, as well as the 25 which preceded it, has been

to teach the content first, and then to write the book. The book becomes an introduction to your Conscious Signature System, and allows you to reach much further than you can without it. If someone buys your book online, they may contact you about having you come to train their staff, taking training from you, or even working with you as a private client. When you speak to a group, you can give the book away or have the organization that hires you purchase a copy for everyone in the audience. That puts it in the hands of not only those who hear you personally, but everyone they influence. And it gives you more credibility as a speaker and expert.

9. **Host a summit and/or live event to broaden your reach** – As we discussed in the chapter on Conscious Communication, nothing better positions you as an expert than speaking to an audience. To grow your Conscious Expert brand and status, do more speaking at professional associations, host your own virtual summit featuring the leading experts in your niche, and/or host your own live 2.5- to 3-day retreats, workshops and events. These all give both people in your tribe and those who are considering becoming part of it a chance to experience you up close and personally. This extended exposure contributes greatly to them knowing, liking, entrusting you, and wanting to hire you for additional premium services.

10. **Train/mentor/certify people to work with you** – Certification is another of our five business models that too few people implement. Yet, it has been the easiest four-figure offer we have sold in my nearly twenty years doing online business. Since you have now created a Conscious Signature System that helps people get results, you have something you could teach other people to do so they can help the people they work with get results. Give your certification a name that is aligned with the name of your Conscious Signature System - and offer it. Some of the people in your community will

have been waiting for that offer, and would not respond to other things you invited them to until you made this available.

11. **Create a next-level offer** – Nearly every transformational process will take people to one level, but there is more ground to navigate. Once people complete your initial process, what is their next level need? For example, there are some people in our community that do not want to oversee the process of having their branding website created – they would love to outsource it. So our premium done-for-you package is perfect for them. As another example, people who graduate from our career coach certification know everything they need to know to coach individuals seeking a job or career change. However, that certification does not teach them how to build a coaching business – so the next level offering is the Conscious Client Attraction Blueprint class or one of our mentoring programs.

For your next level offering, you can either think in terms of their next need and develop a class or program around that, or consider these possibilities.

- Provide done-for-you services
- Do affiliate promotions of value-added services
- Offer licensing opportunities
- Offer branded collateral (t-shirts, pens, etc.)
- Form an association
- Host your own retreat or event to assist with implementation

12. **Acquire other businesses** – Our final scaling strategy, which is the ultimate in hiring the expertise you need, is to purchase other aligned businesses either with similar services. You may either acquire community members, or purchase complementary services that you can add to your offerings. Be sure to work with your legal

counsel when implementing the strategy to avoid violating any securities or other laws.

By applying these 12 strategies, growing your team, and doing your personal work to avoid activating your own Upper Limits, there is literally no limit to the impact you can have in the world.

EPILOGUE

NEXT STEPS

Where do we go from here?

The evolution of consciousness continues, and with your help as a Conscious Expert, it will be infiltrating all aspects of our lives and work in the future!

Know that you have a community of support at marciabench.com and Conscious Experts Academy – and that it will continue growing with your help. See "Your Next Steps" at the end of this book for specific ways you can become an integral part of the Conscious Client Attraction community and engage with us through our events, mentoring and more.

Meanwhile, here are eight shifts you can begin to make – in mindset and action – to integrate Conscious Client Attraction into your everyday life and business.

1. **Shift from short-term strategy to long-term, purpose-based vision.** When you make plans for launches, new programs, and even your daily and weekly tasks, filter them through your life purpose and business vision first. Consider the longer-term effect of your actions as well as your energy.

2. **Shift from general to specific offerings.** Notice whether you are directing your social media posts, emails and other communication to everyone – the wide sweeping view – or just to your *ideal* Tribe

member – the narrow, targeted view. Narrow your focus, grow your income.

3. **Shift from over-customizing to using a reliable Conscious Signature System.** Don't work so hard! Once you have designed a Conscious Signature System you know works, develop new ways to share it and communicate it to its ideal users. Develop a new type of program on the same system – or one part of it - instead of a whole new system.

4. **Shift from individual to group/leveraged services.** If you are getting too busy serving people 1:1, revisit business models 2 through 5 and choose one that will free up your time while letting you serve more people. Record some of your content instead of delivering it all live. Look for ways to leverage in all aspects of your business.

5. **Shift from old style aggressive marketing to new style connection- and relationship-based marketing.** No amount of yellow highlighting and red letters on a page can replace the value of a true connection with a client who knows you value them. Share your story. Show that you can relate to where they are now. Drip content to them and they will reach for it as a thirsty person seeks water in the desert.

6. **Shift from closing sales to enrolling clients.** If you have a background in traditional sales, becoming a Conscious Expert will require updating some of those skills. Trust that as you communicate with the prospect with respect and as an equal, your enrollment percentage will go up. Focus on connecting instead of closing – and you will reap the benefits of both.

7. **Shift from over-promising to over-delivering with your new clients.** People's expectations have dropped as they try to become accustomed to being treated like a number when seeking customer service. WOW them by giving them prompt, high quality service – and they will stay with you for life.

8. **Shift from where you are to your next level of impact – and keep doing it.** Business, like life, is a series of growth cycles. Let go of the beliefs, habits and patterns that got you to your current level of success, even as you envision what's possible and start your leap to the next level. New goals mean new challenges – so seek a mentor that can take you where you want to go.

We'll be with you all the way!

ABOUT THE AUTHOR

Marcia Bench is a best-selling author, professional speaker, intuitive guide and coach. This is her 26th book, and she has been coaching and consulting both individual and corporate clients since 1986.

She's the go-to expert when you want to attract more ideal clients easily and profitably, whether to turn around strategies that aren't working or to leap to the next level of your success. Using Conscious Client Attraction™ and the roadmap of the chakras as her primary marketing approach, Marcia launched her initial business part time, while working as an attorney. It rapidly grew to serve clients in more than 50 countries and has generated more than $2.7 million in revenues. She helps her Conscious Expert clients catapult their impact and their income with her methods as well.

Marcia is CEO of Marcia Bench Enterprises, http://www.marciabench. com, as well as the founder of Career Coach Institute, http://www. careercoachinstitute.com and Conscious Experts Academy, http://www. consciousexpertsacademy.com.

A former attorney, Marcia's previous books include *The Tao of Entrepreneurship: 52 Lessons in Applying Spiritual Principles to Business Ownership, Become an Inspirational Thought Leader, Success by the Numbers,* and *Career Coaching: An Insider's Guide.*

Marcia has been a featured speaker/trainer at hundreds of local, regional and national conferences, as well as on hundreds of webinars. She is a frequent guest on numerous television and radio programs. Her mission is to help visionary coaches, healers, authors, speakers and other entrepreneur experts share their unique gifts with their ideal clients with joy, ease, and financial flow, so they can clearly identify, express, leverage and monetize their life purpose and be fulfilled.

Marcia's coaching experience includes work with managers and executives from Fortune 500 firms in a variety of industries as well as hundreds of business owners, professionals, and military officers entering the civilian workforce.

Prior to entering the expert industry, Marcia was Senior Vice President in a dot-com career management firm for four years, and previously spent ten years as President of New Work Directions, a business and consulting firm she founded. Ms. Bench developed her expertise in business start-up and management in part, through her four years as a practicing attorney, specializing in business and employment issues. She left the law to travel full time for 10 months on a national seminar tour with her first book, taking the risks that she teaches to be a Conscious Expert in action – and she hasn't stopped since.

Marcia's education includes a Juris Doctorate from Northwestern School of Law of Lewis & Clark College and a Bachelor of Science in Psychology from Western Oregon University. In addition, she is a Certified Business Coach, a Certified Teleader and a Master Certified Career Coach. She is a member of Ewomennetwork and Women with Moxie, and is active in many conscious business, coaching, speaking and entrepreneur organizations.

Marcia Bench Enterprises, LLC

29030 SW Town Ctr. Lp. E. #202-454

Wilsonville, OR 97070

www.marciabench.com

(503) 308-8179

CASE STUDIES FEATURED IN THIS BOOK

The case studies and stories featured in this book are the result of hard work and intentional action by each Conscious Expert whose stories you read. They said yes to an opportunity to work closely with me over several months to put the principles of Conscious Client Attraction to the test.

Therefore, I invite you to visit their websites and learn more about their story and what they have to offer.

EXPERT NAME	WEB SITE
Melissa Beaudet	www.career-coach-experts.com
Coach April	www.chronicallywell.org and www.fb.com/glitterqueensglobal
Dr. Lynne Cockrum-Murphy	www.lynnecockrum-murphy.com
Kathy Dempsey	www.kathydempseycoaching.com
Leah Denmark	www.vibrationsoflight.com
Ken Kochajda	www.miaddcareercoach.com
Moses McCutcheon	www.schooltosuccess.com
Germaine Robinson	www.realignmentforwomen.com

YOUR NEXT STEPS

We invite you to visit our website at marciabench.com and subscribe to our Monday Motivation weekly ezine, to learn more about our products, programs, mentoring, workshops and live events.

And we wish you well on your Conscious Client Attraction journey!

CPSIA information can be obtained
at www.ICGtesting.com
Printed in the USA
FSHW020216010221
78087FS

9 781628 655735